THE DECLINE
OF THE WEST?

THE
DECLINE
OF THE WEST?

Edited by MANFRED P. FLEISCHER
University of California, Davis

HOLT, RINEHART AND WINSTON, INC.
New York • Chicago • San Francisco • Atlanta
Dallas • Montreal • Toronto • London • Sydney

Cover illustration: The Roman Forum at Twilight.
(Elliot Erwitt, Magnum)

CONTENTS

AN UNSCIENTIFIC POSTSCRIPT

"The Riders on the Four Horses." Woodcut from the *Apocalypse* by Albrecht Dürer. (From The Metropolitan Museum of Art, Gift of Junius S. Morgan, 1919)

INTRODUCTION

The theories of cultural decline and historical recurrence as well as the practice of prophetic pessimism are rooted in the mythical past of Western civilization. In the Book of Genesis and in Mesopotamian creation stories, the fall of man almost coincides with the making of the world. The Hebrew prophets, the oracle of Delphi, and the Sibylline Books in Rome envisioned the doom of cities and empires, and lest we forget, sooner or later, their prophecies became true. On the basis of Greek mythology, Hesiod (c. 900 B.C.) quartered history into ages of gold, silver, bronze, and iron—a frequent assumption in systems of thought from Plato to Marx.

Among ancient philosophers, the Cynics considered civilization a perversion of natural living conditions, and extolled the unspoiled virtues of primitive people. The Stoics presumed a periodic conflagration of the universe out of which a new world would arise, and repeat the performance. Among ancient historians, the Stoic Polybius (c. 204–122 B.C.) established a circular pattern in which states underwent various forms of government and returned to their origins. Under the emperors Trajan and Hadrian, Florus (c. A.D. 125), an epitomizer of Livy, imposed the Stoic concept of a *cosmopolis* on world history, and divided his biography of Rome into infancy, adolescence, youth, and senility.

According to Hegesippus (c. A.D. 180), fragments of whose "earliest Christian history after the Acts of the Apostles" were preserved by Eusebius, the converter of Constantine, the pristine purity of the church had been polluted by false doctrine right after the death of the disciples. St. Augustine (354–430), as well as his pupil Orosius (c. 385–420), juxtaposed the rising City of God with the falling city of man. Joachim of Floris (c. 1145–1202) felt that the hierarchy of the church as well as the princes of this world would soon go the way of all flesh.

During the Renaissance, the decline theory swung back to the secular side. Petrarch (1304–1374) called the period of pre-Christian Rome *antiqua*—the highest honor this lover of the past could bestow—the age of Constantine, *nova,* and his own time *tenebrae* (shadows) because of the eclipse of the eternal city and the "Babylonian captivity of the church." Flavio Biondo used a descending chronology in his *History from the Decline of the Roman Empire* (1439–1453) starting with Alaric's sack of Rome (A.D. 410, according to Flavio, 412). In Flavio's time

1

table, the "year of salvation" reappeared only in 752 when the rise of the Italian city states promised a recovery of Roman republican virtues. In his *Discourses on the First Ten Books of Livy* (1513), Niccolò Machiavelli discussed the degeneration of governments after the precedent of Polybius, using the same quarry as Florus.

The Protestant Reformation revived the notion of a "fallen church." Lutherans, Calvinists, Anabaptists, Spiritualists, Anti-Trinitarians, and Puritans applied this verdict with increasing radicalism to the Catholic past. The height of this view was expressed in Gottfried Arnold, *Impartial History of the Church and of Heresy* (1699–1700). Arnold recognized none but dissenters as true believers and declared all forms of orthodoxy or organized majority opinion a falling away from the high standards set by Christ and the apostles.

During the Enlightenment, "the silver age to the golden age of the Renaissance," there was a renewed interest in the demise of pagan Rome, the possibility of historical repetition, and the "scientific" prediction of the future. Charles Louis de Montesquieu published *Considerations on the Causes for the Greatness of the Romans and their Decline* (1734). Edward Gibbon wrote *The Decline and Fall of the Roman Empire* (1776–1787).

Giambattista Vico (1668–1744) paralleled corresponding epochs, such as the heroic ages of Homer and medieval chivalry, and suggested that they recurred in the same order. Barbarism begot classicism in which prose replaced poetry; thought, imagination; industry, agriculture; and peace, war. Then, a new "barbarism of reflection" resulted in civil war and party strife, transformed cities into woods, and returned man to the cave. Vico's cycles resembled a coil rather than a wheel, for they advanced sideways. The Christian barbarism of the early Middle Ages was different from its pagan predecessor at the time of the Trojan War. The spiral twist to coming events precluded their prediction.

Beyond the Alps, Vico's *New Science* (1725) was received only when the work of Herder and Hegel created a more congenial atmosphere. But by that time, Antoine Nicolas de Condorcet (1743–1794), "the last of the encyclopedists and most universal of them all," an advocate and victim of the French Revolution, had left a more popular legacy. At the end of his *Sketch for a Historical Picture of the Progress of the Human Mind* (1794), de Condorcet called for a forecast of the future on the basis of the past and found "the strongest reasons for believing that nature has set no limit to the realizations of our hopes."

After the iron age of Napoleon, the nineteenth century followed the lead of de Condorcet, and expected a golden age around the corner. In the trails of Hegel's dialectics, Comte's positivism, or Darwin's evolution, Liberals believed in gradual, Socialists in ultimate progress, taking struggle, setbacks, and dead ends in its stride. Yet, there were "rainpipers" (plovers), as Kierkegaard called himself, attuned to the gathering storm behind the fair weather reports and "full speed ahead" speeches of official optimism. These Cassandras were discovered after Spengler and the current crisis had aroused public concern and scholarly curiosity.

In a sensational speech before the diet in Madrid on January 4, 1849, the Spanish statesman Juan Donoso-Cortés renounced his former liberalism, denounced the revolution of 1848, and predicted an age of dictatorship.

Carl Vollgraff (1792–1863), professor of law and politics at Marburg, Germany, produced the first modern system of historical pessimism.[1] At first sight, Vollgraff's *First Attempt*[2] looks like a caricature of German scholarship. Alas, from its 2500 pages of torturous terminology, floods of footnotes which cover the four corners of the earth, and the constant division of the text by the Pythagorean key figure four, there emerges an amazing anticipation of Spengler.

Vollgraff considered the cultures of the world "a colossal collection of ruins" consisting of civilizations that died long ago; nations that were destroyed in springtime and never grew up to enjoy summer and fall; underdogs who forcibly or voluntarily adopted the culture of a conqueror, and who now were raging in the strait jacket of an alien civilization; and cultural crossbreeds without national origin and ethnic homeland, who cursed their creators.

Among the still living cultures Vollgraff detected the same symptoms that distorted the faces of the dead. There was a loss of faith and fellow feeling, the vulgarization of language, the break with tradition, the disruption of social and family ties, and the lack of cultural creativity, except for the foundation of national libraries and museums, a fading civilization's formation of seed pods. The vanishing of these values which set man apart from the beast started with the most advanced nations and drifted down to the backward. The decline of the West would be hastened by the triumph of science and technology which made work scarce and poverty abundant, by mounting drug addiction (in which Vollgraff included coffee and tea), and by the speed with which people tried to get rich at all costs.

Although Vollgraff based his dance of death on natural law rather than on original sin or tragic guilt, he recognized religion, like Donoso-Cortés, as a barometer of decline. The gods forsook men; and men, their gods. With the power failure of the divine, faith in one's fellow men faded away. Distrust bred hatred and fear. Force formed the new foundation of human and international affairs. Violence would erupt within and among the states and leave on our planet a landscape of the moon.

Ernst von Lasaulx (1815–1861), a Bavarian classics professor and member of parliament, continued Vollgraff's *First Attempt* with a *New Attempt to Base an Old Philosophy of History on the Truth of Facts* (1856) which prepared the

---

[1] This historical school must be distinguished from the philosophical or metaphysical pessimism of Arthur Schopenhauer (1788–1860) and Eduard von Hartmann (1842–1906).

[2] For the full title of this work, which is as untranslatable as the text, see Suggestions for Further Reading, p. 126.

Swiss historian Jakob Burckhardt (1818–1897) for his now widely acknowledged role as prophet of the nineteenth century. Before the German National Assembly in Frankfurt (1848–1849) and the Estates-General in Munich (1849–1852), Lasaulx delivered lectures which duplicated the "speech on dictatorship" by Donoso-Cortés in many details.

Nikolai Danilevsky (1822–1885), a Russian naturalist who served the Czar as an expert on fisheries, published *Russia and Europe* (1869) which became the bible of Panslavism. Danilevsky argued that the West was hostile to Russia, as evidenced by the Crimean War, because she formed a separate Slavic culture. This fact was obscured by the linear arrangement of European history. Just as in biology straight-lined classification had to give way to a cluster of genera and species, so in history the tripartition into ancient, medieval, and modern must be replaced by historicocultural types. Each historicocultural type enjoyed an indefinite time of growth, but its season of flowering and fruitage, relatively short, exhausted it once and for all. The Germano-Romanic civilization of the West had reached the end of its bloom. It would try to subject the Slavs as a fresh source of life. Only Panslavism could beat back the assault and guard the world against European rapacity. Panslavism was destined to supplant European supremacy until it itself would wither, or issue into a world civilization.

Russian critics who pointed out that even Panslavism could not do without the West charged Danilevsky with having taken his historicocultural types as well as the final idea of regeneration toward a world civilization from the *Textbook of World History in Organic Presentation* (1857) by Heinrich Rückert (1823–1875), a professor at the University of Breslau, Germany.

Toward the turn of the century, the philosopher Friedrich Nietzsche (1844–1900) warned that Western civilization was facing a fatal crisis. From the beginning, it had taken the wrong turns. Socrates and Plato promoted "reason" at the expense of "instinct." The apostle Paul imposed a morality on the West which enfeebled the healthy and empowered the sick. Now, the dying faith in the God of truth nursed the nihilistic notion that "all is false," while the secularization of Christian morality by democracy and socialism killed all culture which Nietzsche considered the work of aristocratic values and virtues.

In a similar vein, Vilfredo Pareto mused about the "circulation of the elites." Observing political opportunism, Pareto expected the ladder of popular leadership to tip over, because too many climbed to the top without regard to maintaining equity and equilibrium on the social and economic scale. The revulsion against the lack of principle among the liberal parties would result in a ruthless restoration of "law and order," although Pareto imagined nothing like Mussolini, Hitler, or Stalin.

In the United States, the Adams brothers anticipated the decline of the West. In various books, Brooks Adams foretold the dissolution of the British Empire, the fall of France, as well as the decay of America and with her, Western civilization. Brooks believed modern industrialism used and produced so much "surplus energy" that it would either explode or exhaust itself. Henry Adams (1838–1918), trying to be more scientific, applied a "Rule of Phase" to history. The Mechanical Phase had lasted from 1600 to 1900, the Electric Phase, accelerating itself according to a law of thermodynamics, would last only 17½ years, and the Ethereal Phase, about four. Thought would have reached "the limit of its possibilities in the year 1921."

Oswald Spengler shared this feeling. As a high school teacher of mathematics and natural science, who had earned his Ph.D. with a dissertation on the ancient Greek philosopher Heraclitus, Spengler was alarmed by the blindness of his age to political dangers and the lack of foresight among nations. The second Moroccan crisis (1911) which brought France and Germany to the brink of global war, the *Untergang*[3] of the ship "Titanic" (1912) with its shocking realization that science and technology had not yet mastered the forces of nature, and a voluminous history of the *Untergang* of the ancient world[4] formed the germ cells of his work.

It has been assumed that *The Decline of the West* (1918–1922) was the attempt of a disgruntled German to involve the victorious Allies in his country's defeat. However, the manuscript was finished by 1917 when Russia broke down, and Spengler saw a triumphant Germany in the role of the Roman Empire after the Punic Wars. On the other hand, Spengler's difficult book would have hardly become a bestseller by 1919, if it had not been published at places—first in Vienna, then in Munich—where a world had collapsed.

But again, the title was not intended to spell out disaster. *Der Untergang des Abendlandes* sounds more like "sunset and evening bell." Because our advanced age could no longer create grand opera and great drama, Spengler invited his audience to watch its consummation as South Sea islanders gather on mountain slopes to see the sun go down, and the stars come out. For his "lyric approach"[5] to day and night in the life of mankind Spengler introduced a new music for the historical spheres. Using a figure of speech from astronomy, he discarded the Ptolemaic system within which the West was the center of world history. According to Spengler's Copernican discovery, non-Western cultures, past and present, followed their own circular orbits. The West was only one among six to nine of these separate worlds rising and falling as they did. (Hence the charge of "historical relativism.")

Spengler observed in each culture a succession of birth, growth, maturity, and fulfillment calling the first steps the phase of "culture" and the later ones

---

[3] In German, *Untergang* means the sinking of a ship as well as the setting of the sun. The exact equivalent of decline would be *Niedergang*, to go down but not under.

[4] Otto Seeck, *Geschichte des Unterganges der antiken Welt* (6 vols.; Berlin and Stuttgart, 1895–1921).

[5] James T. Shotwell, "Spengler" in *Essays in Intellectual History,* ed. David Saville Muzzey (New York, 1929), p. 24.

the period of "civilization." (The culture/civilization dichotomy had been used already by J. S. Mill, Vollgraff, and Nietzsche.) Each culture as a whole went through the same stages, and their basic patterns could be arranged side by side or contemporaneously. With such a ground plan one could predict the future of a civilization which had not yet finished its course as well as fill in the gaps in our knowledge of a past culture which had taken its historical records with it.

To do this was the task of a poet who understood the "prime symbols of life" as they came to surface in the course of history and unfolded themselves within a cultural cycle. Nature belonged to the scientist who searched for causes. History dealt with destiny. Day could not be considered the cause of night, and old age was not the effect of youth. Scientific historians who looked for causes and effects in cultural development confused the issues. Moreover, the West was not the scientific measure for the rest of mankind but merely the manifestation of its own destiny.

During famine and inflation "the entire cultured world of Germany made it a point to secure in some way or another this ponderous work"; however, it was almost to a man repudiated by professionals and experts whose fields it touched. The reception of Spengler's historical relativism resembled the initial rejection of Einstein's theory of relativity by his fellow physicists, which occurred about the same time. The facts, however, which Spengler deemed more crucial than truths vindicated his views with a vengeance. Within twenty-five years Europe was ruined by those waves of the future of which Spengler had warned—political mass movements mobilized by the power of the press as well as military and industrial dictators leading the West once more into civil war. When Europe was rebuilt after 1945, it emerged as part of that world city of which Spengler had provided a blueprint in his second volume.

In the intermediate years Spengler's forerunners, most of whom he had not even known himself, reappeared in print, and re-enforced his findings. War and revolution led other writers to similar conclusions. Thus the prophet was suddenly surrounded by a cloud of witnesses whom his detractors dubbed "Spenglerians," although most had made their discoveries independently and saw many things differently.

During the same summer when the *Decline* first appeared, an Hungarian sociologist, C. H. Meray, published in Switzerland a book called *World Mutation* (1918) which treated the causes and consequences of World War I in terms of cancer. Civilizations were similar to cellular organisms, and Europe was suffering its terminal disease.

While Spengler wrote in wartime Munich, Albert Schweitzer had been working on his *Philosophy of Civilization* (1923) in an internment camp in the French Congo. Although of different frames of mind, both Spengler and Schweitzer professed an "elective affinity" for Johann Wolfgang Goethe (1749–1832) and agreed that the West was in trouble.

Arnold J. Toynbee thought that the story of the Peloponnesian War (431–404 B.C.) as told by Thucydides started to repeat itself in August 1914. Toynbee had decided on a comparative study of civilizations when Spengler's publication made him wonder whether his plan had been pre-empted. However, he felt that where German dogmatism drew a blank, work was left for English empiricism. Toynbee increased the number of civilizations; called their life phases genesis, growth, breakdown, and disintegration; and provided the possibility of changing their direction by dint of such modifiers as challenge-and-response or withdrawal-and-return.

Three cyclical decline theories came out of the crucible of the Russian Revolution. Nikolai Berdyaev (1874–1948), who, as a Marxist, had been sent to Siberia under the Czar, was exiled by the Communists because of his conversion to a religious world view. Berdyaev believed that the "humanist-secular" culture of the West would be overcome by "new middle ages." When darkness descended on a dying civilization, its former "stars" at least remained an everlasting possession.

Walter Schubart, a Baltic German who between the wars was a professor in Latvia, continued Danilevsky's combination of cultural history and Panslavicism. According to his *Russia and Western Man* (1938), the "rhythm of world events" was governed by the succession of four prototypes of men: Gothic "harmonious" man who believed he had achieved a balanced society, the ascetic Hindu or neo-Platonist who escaped from the world into the "essence of things," the Promethean hero who all alone attempted to create a cosmos out of chaos, and the Messianic soul who embodied heaven on earth like the "early Christians" and the "majority of Slavs." During the Renaissance and Reformation, Promethean man had destroyed Gothic harmony. Now, the time was ripe for the Messianic age to be ushered in by Russia—"not the present but the future."

Pitirim A. Sorokin, who belonged to the same group of exiles as Berdyaev, and settled in the United States, incorporated the civilizational units of Danilevsky, Spengler, and Toynbee into his "sociocultural supersystems" which exhibited ideational, sensate, and idealistic characteristics. These three states of mind took cyclical turns in the history of every nation, but their duration could not be determined.

The American anthropologist Alfred L. Kroeber measured the rise and decline of creative genius in philosophy, science, philology, sculpture, painting, drama, literature, music, and politics among the world's foremost cultures. Spengler had used innovators chiefly as exemplary illustrations. Kroeber employed them as indicators of cultural phenomena. From their achievement records Kroeber concluded that definite patterns actually appeared in periods of cultural growth. But he wondered whether civilizations developed along parallel lines, and died of themselves.

Another American, the philosopher Filmer S. C. Northrop searched for the sources of cultural conflict and found a basic imbalance between the scientific and theoretical West, and the esthetic and intuitional East. Although Northrop is neither a historical pessimist nor a cyclical theorist but a would-be reducer of international tensions via the dissolution of ideological differences, he shares the physiognomic method with Spengler. Spengler conveyed his cultural cardiograms through the moving pictures of his morphological language. Northrop takes snapshots like a tourist and with the key of his philosophical knowledge deciphers the code of a culture from the facades of its buildings and the figures of its fine arts.

Other members of this cosmopolitan school of cyclical or comparative cultural history will be mentioned in the Suggestions for Further Reading. The phenomenal growth of its literature since 1918 shows that *The Decline of the West* marked a "turning point in historical speculation," as one opponent conceded. "What we must all study today is not the law which governs the progress of societies, but which appears to dictate their decline."[6]

The first two sets of selections feature Hugh Redwald Trevor-Roper, and Pieter Geyl, the harshest critics of the "Spenglerian" concept of world history and its cyclical pattern of the past. Trevor-Roper voices the belief in progress, Geyl echoes the religious skepticism of the Enlightenment. Both pose many questions. Is world history the balance sheet of separate civilizations which rise and fall, a galaxy in which the West is no longer the sun but a shooting star? Or is world history the window dressing of Western civilization? Does the West spearhead the progress of and set the standard for the rest of mankind?

Second, is there a pattern of the past which can be established by the comparative study of civilizations and which is supposed to repeat itself in the future? Or is such determinism a dangerous delusion? How do Sorokin and Toynbee meet the specifications of Spenglerism when they themselves take the stand after their analysis by Geyl?

The third set of selections illustrates (Spengler and Northrop), justifies (Toynbee and B. Adams), and summarizes (Kroeber) some of the methods by which historians and philosophers have tried to grasp the soul, state of mind, or age of a culture.

The fourth set of selections deals with the diagnosis of our crisis. Donoso-Cortés divined dictatorship and the death of liberty when democracy dawned all over Europe. Nietzsche sensed a sudden catastrophe while the civilized world was convinced that it had reached the golden age of security. Pareto explained its precarious existence in a fool's paradise of bourgeois complacency. Spengler announced the "period of the contending states" to a generation which believed it had achieved universal and everlasting peace.

Most contemporaries condemned or ignored these horoscopes, while histo-

---

[6] Douglas Jerrold, *The Lie about the West* (London, 1954), p. 24.

rians declared them unhistorical and unscientific after they appeared to have happened. This raises various questions. Do the features of our crisis, if it is recognized as such, fit the forecasts of cyclical historians and historical pessimists and thus verify their theories? Are their excerpts eye openers, or instances of card stacking, as far as our collection is concerned? Since Danilevsky, Nietzsche, Pareto, and Spengler were accused of having contributed to, or even created the conditions they projected, how can seismographs cause an earthquake?

Fifth, there is a selection of proposed remedies for the present situation, although the agreement on the disease did not produce a consensus concerning the cure. Spengler dismissed projects for the salvation of a dying society as part and parcel of its decline. A second religiousness that caused scientists to leave the laboratory in order to preach panaceas for the ills of the world was only another sign of senility. Schweitzer, however, urged the return to the ethical culture of the eighteenth century and the religious world view of an earlier age. Sorokin charged Schweitzer with prescribing "exactly those Sensate philosophies which, if they did not initiate . . . , at least gave impetus to, an ethical and civilizational decay which became catastrophic, according to Schweitzer, at the middle of the nineteenth century,"[7] and issued an ultimatum for a most radical reorientation. Schubart represents the traditional notion that only a younger nation or new barbarians could redeem an old civilization. Kroeber suggests the reconstitution of the West may have already begun. Eric Hoffer reaffirms the American workingman's faith in his ability to move mountains.

H. Stuart Hughes finally gives a critical estimate of Spengler who supplied the over all title (without question mark) and served as focal point and catalyst of these thoughts in the twentieth century. The epilogue puts the finishing touches on the distinction of the historical, the scientific, and the intuitive.

---

[7] Pitirim A. Sorokin, *Social Philosophies of an Age of Crisis* (Boston, 1950), p. 269.

In the reprinted selections footnotes appearing in the original sources have in general been omitted unless they contribute to the argument or better understanding of the selection.

The Decline of the West, two volumes (1918–1922), by
OSWALD SPENGLER (1880–1936) is essentially a
collection of essays which vary four or five main
themes. But all are based on a new scale of music for
the historical spheres, a cyclical instead of a linear
system, which Spengler called his "Copernican
discovery." Here is the signature, the treble, bass,
and tenor clefs for Spengler's entire composition.*

Oswald Spengler

What Is World History?

Thanks to the subdivision of history
into "Ancient," "Mediaeval" and "Modern—an incredibly jejune and *meaningless* scheme, which has, however, entirely
dominated our historical thinking—we
have failed to perceive the true position
in the general history of higher mankind
of the little part-world which has developed on West European soil from the time
of the German-Roman Empire, to judge
of its relative importance and above all to
estimate its direction. The Cultures that
are to come will find it difficult to believe
that the validity of such a scheme with its
simple rectilinear progression and its
meaningless proportions, becoming more
and more preposterous with each century,

incapable of bringing into itself the new
fields of history as they successively come
into the light of our knowledge, was, in
spite of all, never wholeheartedly attacked. It is not only that the scheme cir-
cumscribes the area of history. What is
worse, it rigs the stage. The Western
European area is regarded as a fixed pole,
a unique patch chosen on the surface of
the sphere for no better reason, it seems,
than because we live on it—and great histories of millennial duration and mighty
faraway Cultures are made to revolve
around this pole in all modesty. It is a
quaintly conceived system of sun and
planets! We select a single bit of ground as
the natural centre of the historical system,

and make it the central sun. From it all the events of history receive their real light; from it their importance is judged in *perspective*.

It is self-evident that for the Cultures of the West the existence of Athens, Florence or Paris is more important than that of Loyang or Pataliputra. But is it permissible to found a scheme of world-history on estimates of such a sort? If so, then the Chinese historian is quite entitled to frame a world-history in which the Crusades, the Renaissance, Caesar and Frederick the Great are passed over in silence as insignificant. How, *from the morphological point of view*, should our eighteenth century be more important than any other of the sixty centuries that preceded it? Is it not ridiculous to oppose a "modern" history of a few centuries, and that history to all intents localized in West Europe, to an "ancient" history which covers as many millennia—incidentally dumping into that "ancient history" the whole mass of the pre-Hellenic cultures, unprobed and unordered, as mere appendix-matter? This is no exaggeration. Do we not, for the sake of keeping the hoary scheme, dispose of Egypt and Babylon—each as an individual and self-contained history quite equal in the balance to our so-called "world-history" from Charlemagne to the World War and well beyond it—as a *prelude* to Classical history? Do we not relegate the vast complexes of Indian and Chinese Culture to footnotes, with a gesture of embarrassment? As for the great American Cultures, do we not, on the ground that they do not "fit in" (with what?), entirely ignore them?

The most appropriate designation for this current West European scheme of history, in which the great Cultures are made to follow orbits round us as the presumed centre of all world-happenings, is the *Ptolemaic system* of history. The system

that is put forward in this work in place of it I regard as the *Copernican discovery* in the historical sphere, in that it admits no sort of privileged position to the Classical or the Western Culture as against the Cultures of India, Babylon, China, Egypt, the Arabs, Mexico—separate worlds of dynamic being which in point of mass count for just as much in the general picture of history as the Classical, while frequently surpassing it in point of spiritual greatness and soaring power.

The scheme "ancient-mediaeval-modern" in its first form was a creation of the Magian world-sense. It first appeared in the Persian and Jewish religions after Cyrus, received an apocalyptic sense in the teaching of the Book of Daniel on the four world-eras and was developed into a world-history in the post-Christian religions of the East, notably the Gnostic systems.

This important conception, within the very narrow limits which fixed its intellectual basis, was unimpeachable. Neither Indian nor even Egyptian history was included in the scope of the proposition. For the Magian thinker the expression "world-history" meant a unique and supremely dramatic act, having as its theatre the lands between Hellas and Persia, in which the strictly dualistic world-sense of the East expressed itself not by means of polar conceptions like the "soul and spirit," "good and evil" of contemporary metaphysics, but by the figure of a catastrophe, an epochal change of phase between world-creation and world-decay. No elements beyond those which we find stabilized in the Classical literature, on the one hand, and the Bible (or other sacred book of the particular system), on the other, came into the picture, which presents (as "the Old" and "the New," respectively) the easily grasped contrasts of Gentile and Jewish, Christian and Heathen,

Classical and Oriental, idol and dogma, nature and spirit *with a time connotation* —that is, as a drama in which the one prevails over the other. The historical change of period wears the characteristic dress of the religious "Redemption." This "world-history" in short was a conception narrow and provincial, but within its limits logical and complete. Necessarily, therefore, it was specific to this region and this humanity, and incapable of any *natural* extension.

But to these two there has been added a third epoch, the epoch that we call "modern," on Western soil, and it is this that for the first time gives the picture of history the look of a progression. The oriental picture was *at rest*. It presented a self-contained antithesis, with equilibrium as its outcome and a unique divine act as its turning-point. But, adopted and assumed by a wholly new type of mankind, it was quickly transformed (without anyone's noticing the oddity of the change) into a conception of a *linear progress:* from Homer or Adam—the modern can substitute for these names the Indo-German, Stone Age, or the Pithecanthropus—through Jerusalem, Rome, Florence and Paris according to the taste of the individual historian, thinker or artist, who has unlimited freedom in the interpretation of the three-part scheme.

This third term, "modern times," which in form asserts that it is the last and conclusive term of the series, has in fact, ever since the Crusades, been stretched and stretched again to the elastic limit at which it will bear no more. It was at least implied, if not stated in so many words, that here, beyond the ancient and the mediaeval, something definitive was beginning, a Third Kingdom in which, somewhere, there was to be fulfilment and culmination, and which had an objective point. As to what this objective point is,

each thinker, from Schoolman to present-day Socialist, backs his own peculiar discovery.

On the very threshold of the Western Culture we meet the great Joachim of Floris (c. 1145–1202), the first thinker of the Hegelian stamp, who shattered the dualistic world-form of Augustine, and with his essentially Gothic intellect stated the new Christianity of his time in the form of a third term to the religions of the Old and the New Testaments, expressing them respectively as the Age of the Father, the Age of the Son and the Age of the Holy Ghost. His teaching moved the best of the Franciscans and the Dominicans, Dante, Thomas Aquinas, in their inmost souls and awakened a world-outlook which slowly but surely took entire possession of the historical sense of our Culture. Lessing—who often designated his own period with reference to the Classical as the "after-world" *(Nachwelt)*—took his idea of the "education of the human race," with its three stages of child, youth and man, from the teaching of the fourteenth-century mystics. Ibsen treats it with thoroughness in his *Emperor and Galilean* (1873), in which he directly presents the Gnostic world-conception through the figure of the wizard Maximus, and advances not a step beyond it in his famous Stockholm address of 1887. It would appear, then, that the Western consciousness feels itself urged to predicate a sort of finality inherent in its own appearance.

But the creation of the Abbot of Floris was a *mystical* glance into the secrets of the divine world-order. It was bound to lose all meaning as soon as it was used in the way of reasoning and made a hypothesis of *scientific* thinking, as it has been— ever more and more frequently—since the seventeenth century.

It is a quite indefensible method of presenting world-history to begin by giving rein to one's own religious, political or social convictions and endowing the sacrosanct three-phase system with tendencies that will bring it exactly to one's own standpoint. This is, in effect, making of some formula—say, the "Age of Reason," Humanity, the greatest happiness of the greatest number, enlightenment, economic progress, national freedom, the conquest of nature or world-peace—a criterion whereby to judge whole millennia of history. And so we judge that they were ignorant of the "true path," or that they failed to follow it, when the fact is simply that their will and purposes were not the same as ours. Goethe's saying "What is important in life is life and not a result of life" is the answer to any and every senseless attempt to solve the riddle of historical form by means of a *programme.*

It is the same picture that we find when we turn to the historians of each special art or science (and those of national economics and philosophy as well). We find:

"Painting" from the Egyptians (or the cavemen) to the Impressionists, or

"Music" from Homer to Bayreuth and beyond, or

"Social Organization" from Lake Dwellings to Socialism, as the case may be,

presented as a linear graph which steadily rises in conformity with the values of the (selected) arguments. No one has seriously considered the possibility that arts may have an allotted span of life and may be attached as forms of self-expression to particular regions and particular types of mankind, and that therefore the total history of an art may be merely an additive compilation of separate developments, of special arts, with no bond of union save the name and some details of craft-technique.

We know it to be true of every organism that the rhythm, form and duration of its life, and all the expression-details of that life as well, are determined by the *properties of its species.* No one, looking at the oak, with its millennial life, dare say that it is at this moment, now, about to start on its true and proper course. No one as he sees a caterpillar grow day by day expects that it will go on doing so for two or three years. In these cases we feel, with an unqualified certainty, a *limit,* and this sense of the limit is identical with our sense of the inward form. In the case of higher human history, on the contrary, we take our ideas as to the course of the future from an unbridled optimism that sets at naught all historical, i.e. *organic,* experience, and everyone therefore sets himself to discover in the accidental present terms that he can expand into some striking progression-series, the existence of which rests not on scientific proof but on predilection.

"Mankind," however, has no aim, no idea, no plan, any more than the family of butterflies or orchids. "Mankind" is a zoological expression, or an empty word. But conjure away the phantom, break the magic circle, and at once there emerges an astonishing wealth of *actual* forms—the Living with all its immense fullness, depth and movement—hitherto veiled by a catchword, a dry-as-dust scheme and a set of personal "ideals." I see, in place of that empty figment of *one* linear history which can be kept up only by shutting one's eyes to the overwhelming multitude of the facts, the drama of *a number* of mighty Cultures, each springing with primitive strength from the soil of a mother-region to which it remains firmly bound throughout its whole life-cycle; each stamping its material, its mankind, in *its own* image; each having *its own* idea, *its own* passions, *its own* life, will and feeling, *its own* death. Here indeed are colours, lights, movements, that no intellectual eye has yet discovered. Here the

Cultures, peoples, languages, truths, gods, landscapes bloom and age as the oaks and the pines, the blossoms, twigs and leaves—but there is no aging "Mankind." Each Culture has its own new possibilities of self-expression which arise, ripen, decay and never return. There is not *one* sculpture, *one* painting, *one* mathematics, *one* physics, but many, each in its deepest essence different from the others, each limited in duration and self-contained, just as each species of plant has its peculiar blossom or fruit, its special type of growth and decline. These Cultures, sublimated life-essences, grow with the same superb aimlessness as the flowers of the field. They belong, like the plants and the animals, to the living Nature of Goethe, and not to the dead Nature of Newton. I see world-history as a picture of endless formations and transformations, of the marvellous waxing and waning of organic forms. The professional historian, on the contrary, sees it as a sort of tapeworm industriously adding onto itself one epoch after another.

But the series "ancient-mediaeval-modern history" has at last exhausted its usefulness. Angular, narrow, shallow though it was as a scientific foundation, still we possessed no other form that was not wholly unphilosophical in which our data could be arranged, and world-history (as hitherto understood) has to thank it for filtering our classifiable solid residues. But the number of centuries that the scheme can by any stretch be made to cover has long since been exceeded, and with the rapid increase in the volume of our historical material—especially of material that cannot possibly be brought under the scheme—the picture is beginning to dissolve into a chaotic blur.

HUGH REDWALD TREVOR-ROPER (b. 1914), since 1957 regius professor at Oxford, became widely known through his work *The Last Days of Hitler* (1947) based on his detective duties as a British intelligence officer. He edited Hitler's war directives and table talks as well as English poetry and published books and essays on the Reformation era and the age of European expansion. Too late for lancing Spengler, Trevor-Roper lampooned "Arnold Toynbee's Millennium" (see Suggestions for Further Reading) and with the words, "Let us hear no more of the Decline of the West," condemned the whole "doctrine of messianic defeatism."*

Hugh Redwald Trevor-Roper

The Stages of Progress

It is fashionable to speak today as if European history were devalued: as if historians, in the past, have paid too much attention to it; and as if, nowadays, we should pay less. Undergraduates, seduced, as always, by the changing breath of journalistic fashion, demand that they should be taught the history of black Africa. Perhaps, in the future, there will be some African history to teach. But at present there is none, or very little: there is only the history of the Europeans in Africa. The rest is largely darkness, like the history of pre-European, pre-Columbian America. And darkness is not a subject for history.

Please do not misunderstand me. I do not deny that men existed even in dark countries and dark centuries, nor that they had political life and culture, interesting to sociologists and anthropologists; but history, I believe, is essentially a form of movement, and purposive movement too. It is not a mere phantasmagoria of changing shapes and costumes, of battles and conquests, dynasties and usurpations, social forms and social disintegration. If all history is equal, as some now believe, there is no reason why we should study one section of it rather than another; for certainly we cannot study it all. Then indeed we may neglect our own history and amuse ourselves with the unrewarding gyrations of barbarous tribes in picturesque but irrelevant corners of the globe: tribes whose chief function in history, in

*From *The Rise of Christian Europe* by Hugh Trevor-Roper, © copyright, 1965, by Thames and Hudson, London. Reprinted by permission of Harcourt, Brace & World, Inc. Pp. 9–11. This is published in Canada and Britain by Thames and Hudson Ltd.

my opinion, is to show to the present an image of the past from which, by history, it has escaped; or shall I seek to avoid the indignation of the medievalists by saying, from which it has changed?

For on this subject, I believe, with the great historians of the eighteenth century, whom I find very good company (the good sense of the ancients is often more illuminating than the documented ped-antry of the moderns), that history, or rather the study of history, has a purpose. We study it not merely for amusement—though it can be amusing—but in order to discover how we have come to where we are. In the eighteenth century men cer-tainly studied Afro-Asian *society*. Turn over the pages of the great French and Scottish writers—Montesquieu, Voltaire, Hume, Adam Smith, Millar. Their inter-est in non-European society is obvious. Indeed, in order to found the new science of sociology—one of the great intellectual contributions of the Enlightenment—they turned deliberately away from Europe. They read the accounts of European mis-sionaries and drew general deductions from the customs of Otaheite and the Caribbees. But with Afro-Asian history, as distinct from society, they had little pa-tience. When Dr Johnson bestowed exces-sive praise on a certain old *History of the Turks,* Gibbon pulled him up sharply: "An enlightened age," he replied, would not be satisfied with "1,300 folio pages of speeches and battles": it "requires from the historian some tincture of philosophy and criticism." "If all you have to tell us," said Voltaire, in his advice to contempo-rary historians, "is that one barbarian suc-ceeded another barbarian on the banks of the Oxus or the Jaxartes, what benefit have you conferred on the public?" And David Hume, pushing his way briskly through "the obscure and uninteresting period of the Saxon annals," remarked

that it was "fortunate for letters" that so much of the barbarous detail was "buried in silence and oblivion." "What instruc-tion or entertainment can it give the reader" he asked "to hear a long bead-roll of barbarous names, Egric, Annas, Ethel-bert, Ethelwald, Aldulf, Elfwold, Beorne, Ethelred, Ethelbert, who successively murdered, expelled, or inherited from each other, and obscurely filled the throne" of East Anglia? This is not to say that Hume was indifferent to problems of Anglo-Saxon society. His brilliant appen-dix on that subject disproves any such suggestion. But he distinguished between society and history. To him, as to all these writers, whig or tory, radical or conserva-tive, the positive content of history con-sisted not in the meaningless fermenta-tion of passive or barbarous societies but in the movement of society, the process, conscious or unconscious, by which cer-tain societies, at certain times, had risen out of the barbarism once common to all, and, by their efforts and example, by the interchange and diffusion of arts and sciences, gradually drawn or driven other societies along with them to "the full light and freedom of the eighteenth century."

Today, though it is fashionable to be more sceptical about the light and free-dom, I do not think that the essential func-tion of history has changed. And if the function has not changed, the substance has not changed either. It may well be that the future will be the future of non-European peoples: that the "colonial" peoples of Africa and Asia will inherit that primacy in the world which the "im-perialist" West can no longer sustain. Such shifts in the centre of political grav-ity in the world, such replacement of im-perialist powers by their former colonies, have often happened in the past. Mediter-ranean Europe was once, in the Dark Ages, a colony of Islam; and northern

Europe was afterwards, in the Middle Ages, a colony of the Mediterranean. But even if that should happen, it would not alter the past. The new rulers of the world, whoever they may be, will inherit a position that has been built up by Europe, and by Europe alone. It is European techniques, European examples, European ideas which have shaken the non-European world out of its past—out of barbarism in Africa, out of a far older, slower, more majestic civilization in Asia; and the history of the world, for the last five centuries, in so far as it has significance, has been European history. I do not think we need make any apology if our study of history is Europa-centric.

Another mainstay of OSWALD SPENGLER was his morphology. Morphology is a branch of biology which deals with the form and structure of animals and plants. Spengler considered cultures organic structures that unfolded the forms of growth, flowering, fruitage, and fading while they completed their life cycles. For this insight Spengler gave credit to Goethe whose intuitive mind had comprehended the perennial process as a whole and closed a gap in anatomical knowledge by correlating in man and animals a certain jawbone, the *premaxilla* or *os intermaxillare,* also called "Goethe's bone," on the basis of his form-fulfillment theory.*

Oswald Spengler

Cultures as Organisms

The deep, and scarcely appreciated, idea of Goethe, which he discovered in his "living nature" and always made the basis of his morphological researches, we shall here apply—in its most precise sense—to all the formations of man's history, whether fully matured, cut off in the prime, half opened or stifled in the seed. It is the method of living into *(erfühlen)* the object, as opposed to dissecting it. "The highest to which man can attain, is wonder; and if the prime phenomenon makes him wonder, let him be content; nothing higher can it give him, and nothing further should he seek for behind it; here is the limit." The prime phenomenon is that in which the idea of becoming is presented net. To the spiritual eye of Goethe the idea of the prime plant was clearly visible in the form of every individual plant that happened to come up, or even that could possibly come up. In his investigation of the "os intermaxillare" his starting-point was the *prime phenomenon of the vertebrate type;* and in other fields it was geological stratification, of the leaf as the prime form of the plant-organism, or the metamorphosis of the plants as the prime form of all organic becoming. "The same law will apply to everything else that lives," he wrote, in announcing his discovery to Herder. It was a look into the heart of things that Leibniz would have understood, but the century of Darwin is as remote from such a vision as it is possible to be.

At present, however, we look in vain for any treatment of history that is entirely free from the methods of Darwinism—that is, of systematic natural science based on causality. A physiognomic that is precise, clear and sure of itself and its limits has never yet arisen, and it can only arise through the discoveries of method that we have yet to make. Herein lies the great problem set for the twentieth century to solve—to explore carefully the inner structure of the organic units through and in which world-history fulfils itself, to separate the morphologically necessary from the accidental, and, by seizing the *purport* of events, to ascertain the languages in which they speak.

A boundless mass of human Being, flowing in a stream without banks; upstream, a dark past wherein our time-sense loses all powers of definition and restless or uneasy fancy conjures up geological periods to hide away an eternally unsolvable riddle; downstream, a future even so dark and timeless—such is the groundwork of the Faustian picture of human history.

Over the expanse of the water pass the endless uniform ripples of the generations. Here and there bright shafts of light broaden out, everywhere dancing flashes confuse and disturb the clear mirror, changing, sparkling, vanishing. These are what we call the clans, tribes, peoples, races which unify a series of generations within this or that limited area of the historical surface. As widely as these differ in creative power, so widely do the images that they create vary in duration and plasticity, and when the creative power dies out, the physiognomic, linguistic and spiritual identification-marks vanish also and the phenomenon subsides again into the ruck of the generations. Aryans, Mongols, Germans, Celts, Parthians, Franks, Carthaginians, Berbers, Bantus, are names by which we specify some very heterogeneous images of this order.

But over this surface, too, the great Cultures accomplish their majestic wave-cycles. They appear suddenly, swell in splendid lines, flatten again and vanish, and the face of the waters is once more a sleeping waste.

A Culture is born in the moment when a great soul awakens out of the proto-spirituality of ever-childish humanity, and detaches itself, a form from the formless, a bounded and mortal thing from the boundless and enduring. It blooms on the soil of an exactly definable landscape, to which plant-wise it remains bound. It dies when this soul has actualized the full sum of its possibilities in the shape of peoples, languages, dogmas, arts, states, sciences, and reverts into the proto-soul. But its living existence, that sequence of great epochs which define and display the stages of fulfilment, is an inner passionate struggle to maintain the Idea against the powers of Chaos without and the unconscious muttering deep down within. It is not only the artist who struggles against the resistance of the material and the stifling of the idea within him. Every Culture stands in a deeply symbolical, almost in a mystical, relation to the Extended, the space, in which and through which it strives to actualize itself. The aim once attained—the idea, the entire content of inner possibilities, fulfilled and made externally actual—the Culture suddenly hardens, it mortifies, its blood congeals, its force breaks down, and it becomes *Civilization*, the thing which we feel and understand in the words Egypticism, Byzantinism, Mandarinism. As such it may, like a worn-out giant of the primeval forest, thrust decaying branches towards the sky for hundreds or thousands of years, as we see in China, in India, in the Islamic world. It was thus that the Classical Civilization rose gigantic, in the Imperial age, with a false semblance of youth and strength and fullness, and robbed the young Arabian Culture of the East of light and air.

This—the inward and outward fulfilment, the finality, that awaits every living Culture—is the purport of all the historic "declines," amongst them that decline of the Classical which we know so well and fully, and another decline, entirely comparable to it in course and duration, which will occupy the first centuries of the coming millennium but is heralded already and sensible in and around us today—the decline of the West. Every Culture passes through the age-phases of the individual man. Each has its childhood, youth, manhood and old age. It is a young and trembling soul, heavy with misgivings, that reveals itself in the morning of Romanesque and Gothic. It fills the Faustian landscape from the Provence of the troubadours to the Hildesheim cathedral of Bishop Bernward.[1] The spring wind blows over it. Childhood speaks to us also—and in the same tones—out of early-Homeric Doric, out of early-Christian (which is really early-Arabian) art and out of the works of the Old Kingdom in Egypt that began with the Fourth Dynasty. A mythic world-consciousness is fighting like a harassed debtor against all the dark and daemonic in itself and in Nature, while slowly ripening itself for the pure, day-bright expression of the existence that it will at last achieve and know. The more nearly a Culture approaches the noon culmination of its being, the more virile, austere, controlled, intense the form-language it has secured for itself, the more assured its sense of its own power, the clearer its lineaments. We find every individual trait of expression deliberate, strict, measured, marvellous in its ease and self-confidence, and everywhere, at moments, the coming fulfilment suggested. Still later, tender to the point of fragility, fragrant with the sweetness of late October days, come the Cnidian Aphrodite and the Hall of the Maidens in the Erechtheum, the arabesques on Saracen horseshoe-arches, the Zwinger of Dresden, Watteau, Mozart. At last, in the grey dawn of Civilization, the fire in the soul dies down. The dwindling powers rise to one more, half-successful, effort of creation, and produce the Classicism that is common to all dying Cultures. The soul thinks once again, and in Romanticism looks back piteously to its childhood; then finally, weary, reluctant, cold, it loses its desire to be, and, as in Imperial Rome, wishes itself out of the overlong daylight and back in the darkness of proto-mysticism, in the womb of the mother, in the grave.

---

[1] St. Bernward was Bishop of Hildesheim from 993 to 1022, and himself architect and metal-worker. Three other churches besides the cathedral survive in the city from his time or that of his immediate successors, and Hildesheim of all North German cities is richest in monuments of the Romanesque.

PIETER GEYL (1887–1966) was London
correspondent of a Dutch newspaper (1914–1919),
professor of Dutch history at University College in
London (1919–1935), and finally professor at the
University of Utrecht in his homeland. After World
War II, the worst part of which he spent in forced
retirement, Geyl turned his attention to problems of
historiography. In a discussion with Arnold J. Toynbee
programmed by the British Broadcasting Corporation
in 1948, he openly questioned the common pattern of
different cultures, which was supposed to be shown in
the first six volumes of Toynbee's *Study of History*
(1934–1939), and continued to do so in later essays. Geyl
became more and more convinced that Toynbee was a
"new Spenglerian" and together with Sorokin, a
"prophet of woe."*

Pieter Geyl

Sorokin and Toynbee
"Prophets of Woe"

Pessimism about the prospect of our
civilization is wide-spread. It is unnecessary to recapitulate the circumstances of
modern life and the symptoms of its unrest which form the stock-in-trade of the
pessimists. One might say the distur-
bances fall into two categories. There are
the social phenomena which accompany
the immense social transformations
through which we are all passing—the
disintegration of the middle classes and
the rise of the working classes: two sides
of the same leveling process in which it
is possible—it all depends on the point of
view one takes—to discern above all the
spread of material welfare and cultural
opportunities among the masses of mankind. And there are, of course, not only
the social transformations occurring in

the various Caucasian countries of Western civilization, but there are also the shifts
in the relationship between the colored
peoples, the Asiatic peoples in particular,
and the white world. This along with the
rising power of the working classes
strikes many of the once dominant race
as an incident, although a particularly
ominous one. It is seen as the uprising
of the mob, "the revolt of the masses,"
as Ortega y Gasset put it in his famous
book. My quotation of this well-known
phrase will serve as a reminder that
the mood of pessimism which I am discussing was no product of the war; it
existed among intellectuals before the
war, although there is no doubt that the
war intensified it. Not only have both
world wars heightened this mood of fu-

tility—wars usually have the effect of speeding up the process of history—but they have, moreover, created difficulties and dangers and fears of their own. But it is not my intention to go into these problems independently. What I want to do is discuss one favorite method of the prophets of woe—the historical method, the appeal to the past.

It is, I suppose, an ingrained habit of the human mind and indeed it is a noble ambition—to try to construct a vision of history in which chaos, or apparent chaos, is reduced to order. The historical process is made to conform to a line, a rhythm, a regularity—a movement, in other words, which obeys definable and intelligible laws and which can, therefore, be predicted by the observer beyond the moment of his own life. It used to be fashionable in the eighteenth and nineteenth centuries to do this in a spirit of optimism. People were sure then that history was but the record of steady progress. They were entirely complacent about their own time when they looked back at the past, but they had no doubt that succeeding generations would be even happier, even richer, and even wiser and more enlightened than they were themselves. The spirit of optimism has somehow evaporated, but the men who now give expression to the prevailing mood, frequently, like their optimistic predecessors, base their views on a comtemplation of the past. Only the past now takes on a rosy hue, and its interpreters like especially to take their stand on some historical system which no longer shows the straight line of progress, but is generally composed of recurring cycles. Their important point is to demonstrate that our generation, our civilization, has reached about the last and lowest stage of one such cycle and that, consequently, disaster lies immediately ahead.

What I propose to do is to examine the methods employed in some of these demonstrations, and especially to test the way in which history is made to serve the purpose of the demonstrators.

I shall deal with two well-known contemporary writers only: namely, with Professor Sorokin of Harvard, and his enormous four-volume work, "Social and Cultural Dynamics," and with Arnold Toynbee and his no less enormous (but far more readable!) six-volume "Study of History." Both men were profoundly influenced by Oswald Spengler, whose "Decline of the West" made such an impression after the First World War. It is tempting to say something more on that powerful work, but I will only point out that the influence I am concerned with is not so much the general one of the great synthesis buttressing up a gloomy view of the future, as more particularly the way in which Spengler pictures civilizations as independent and mutually impenetrable entities. This is one of the basic elements of his system. He compares civilizations—one might almost say he identifies them—with living organisms. Like them, they pass through the stages of youth, vigorous middle age, old age, and senility, to inevitable dissolution. A civilization is made to appear a living being with an identity and a history of its own, its human components no more able than are the blood particles or the tissues of a human body to stop or to deflect this course laid down by the inexorable laws of nature. Comparisons are, of course, always permissible and they are a powerful aid to the imagination, but there are peculiar dangers attached to them; they should be handled with caution. Nothing can be more misleading than the suggestion that an identity exists between the processes of history and those of organic nature. In that identification the human factor is overlooked, and it is with the human factor that history is, above all, concerned—or should be.

When I suggest that Sorokin and Toynbee have been influenced by Spengler in this matter, I do not mean that they have been blind to this particular pitfall.

II

Professor Sorokin tries in his four bulky tomes to establish a system of the dynamics of culture. This impressive work is an attempt to apply the methods of sociology to the past. He arrives at a classification of civilizations which falls into two main types: the ideational and the sensate. The first posits reality as nonmaterial and everlasting, its needs and ends being mainly spiritual; the sensate culture, on the other hand, thinks of reality as becoming, progress, change, flux, evolution, transformation, its needs and aims being mainly physical. Each of these civilizations traverses, according to Sorokin, a number of stages, from adolescence to maturity and decay. One is very forcibly reminded of Spengler here. Yet at first Sorokin seems to make large concessions to the objections which are bound to come from the historian—the historian who has his attention primed for the endless variety of reality, for the particularity or singularity of each country, of each age, and, more than that, of each incident or phenomenon within these larger frameworks. Sorokin admits that there is an infinite number of cultural types which can be empirically observed. But, he says, this is chaos. His classification, which he asserts is logically satisfactory, helps to arrange the phenomena in an order. But none of his types, he admits this too, has ever existed in a pure form. He even goes so far as to deny the existence of civilizations as really cohesive systems, subject to change in their entirety. These considerations, which he develops with great acumen and sociological learning, cut at the roots of any attempt (or so one should have thought) to make the movements of cultural phenomena conform to regular and predictable lines.

Yet this does not prevent Sorokin from ending on a very positive note. He has by then, to his own satisfaction, identified our present-day civilization as "a typically *sensate* culture in its post-mature stage," and, apparently basing himself on all the statistics, graphs, and analyses in the preceding two and a half thousand pages, he formulates a very definite and depressing prognostication.

"Rude force and cynical fraud"—I quote from the predictions which he lists in his conclusion: this is the fifth one—"will become the only values in all interindividual and inter-group relationships."

"Freedom"—this is his sixth point—"will become a mere myth for the majority." Of course everybody with some perception of the present world and not wilfully blind to disagreeable symptoms knows that these are our dangers, although the historian will soon reflect that it is by no means the first time the world has been threatened with them. But there were always crosscurrents, signs of resistance, of recovery, of fight. And are there none such today? Why should we not look to these phenomena for the true indications of our future? If Professor Sorokin thinks he is in a position to prophesy, is it not because in the end he has succumbed to his own classification, and has accepted as absolute and compelling in objective reality what he began by telling us was only a device intended to bring clarity into the appearance of chaos which history presented to his mind?

It was only the other day that I came across the following passage in the prewar book of an English historian. After some skeptical remarks on "philosophies of history," Mr. E.M. Young admits the existence of facts "which dominate the system" (of history). "But," he continues, "if we ask what this system is, which provides our canon of valuation, I do not believe we can . . . go further than to say, it is the picture as the individual observer sees it. If we trespass across this boundary, we may find ourselves insensibly succumbing to one of the most insidious vices of the human mind; what the Germans in their terse and sparkling way call: the *hypostatization of methodological categories,* or: the habit of treating a mental convenience as if it were an objective thing."

I am afraid that this is exactly what Professor Sorokin is doing, and the impression is much strengthened when one takes a critical look at the structure of fact and argument on which he bases his conclusions. Nobody can help being awed by the immense labor that is involved. Scores of scholars all over the United States and Europe have assisted in compiling statistics. The numbers of casualties in wars over twenty-five centuries have been estimated and compared; and so have the numbers of books or of paintings showing a prevalent percentage either of *sensate* or of *ideational* characteristics in any given period. I must say that these immensely elaborate tables strike me as entirely unconvincing. To me it seems an illusion to think that so complicated, so many-sided, so protean and elusive a thing as a civilization can be reduced to the bare and simple language of rows of figures. The idea that by such a device the subjective factor in the final judgment can be eliminated, is the worst illusion of all. The criteria by which the classifications are to be made cannot really reduce the humblest assistant to a machine (for much

work is often left to assistants as if it were something mechanical or impersonal). When it comes to comparative statistics ranging over the whole history of the human race, does not Sorokin forget how scanty are the data for some periods, how unmanageably abundant for others? Is it possible, in the statistical method, to guard against the difficulty presented by the fact that what survives from the remote past are mostly the thoughts and works of art of an élite, while in our view of our own age, the activities and idiosyncracies of the multitude take an infinitely larger, but perhaps a disproportionate, place? A balance has to be struck between these and many other aspects of history; that is to say, between the records of human activities in many countries and in many ages, that are so scrappy, or again so full, so dissimilar, and mutually impossible to equate. The question imposes itself: Can anybody, in attempting this, claim that he is guided by the sure methods of science? Can he embrace with his mind the whole of that immense chaos and derive from it a conclusion which would be evident to every other human intellect, as would a proposition in Euclid?

I doubt it, or rather—I deny it. I said a moment ago that Professor Sorokin had fallen a victim to his own system and had ended by accepting his classifications as objective and compelling facts. Is it not rather than he *began* with a conviction and then set out to prove it? Most of his imposing and abundant array of facts and figures, in other words, is really irrelevant. If one wishes a sidelight on the value of Sorokin's statistics, which are supposed to tabulate and fix the evidence of literature as well as of all other matters, one has only to read the pages where he lets himself go and confides to us his opinions about literature. He appears to have private and spontaneous opinions—

and of course the statistics never contradict these. But it is interesting to note what he has to say on his own hook. The decline of literature due to the hypertrophy of the sensate factor apparently began in the eighteenth century, and the lover of old English fiction will be surprised to learn that Richardson and Fielding were pessimists, who could sketch in their novels only insignificant characters, failures, or negative types. What can be the worth of a system of ultimate values when the statistics on which it is allegedly built have not saved the author from misapprehensions so patent to anybody who simply has read the writers in question? Sorokin is much concerned, also, about the debunking tendency in historiography. Even Lincoln, he says, is not spared, and he considers this to be an ominous symptom. But, I am inclined to think, the debunking fashion was never more than a passing phase, from which not too much should be deduced about the state of Western civilization. And as regards Lincoln—we have recently had Sandburg, we are still getting Randall. The debunking phase seems closed, and must we now conclude that Western civilization is saved? But for Sorokin—and this is the point I want to make—the conclusion that Western civilization is in a decline, owing to a surfeit of materialism and other evils, was the one point fixed and determined beforehand. Modern literature or modern art or the state of modern society do not really compel him to conclude that our civilization is doomed; his conviction that this is so colors throughout, statistics or no statistics, his view of literature, of art, of the state of society, and of everything else.

III

Professor Toynbee has reacted in his own way against the influence of Spengler —and he has reacted very strongly. He rejects expressly and emphatically the master's identification of civilizations with living organisms. The life of a civilization is not necessarily subject to a decline, it is not subject (as he puts it) to the "iron necessity" of dissolution. It all depends on the energy and the efficiency with which the members of a civilization respond to the challenge with which that civilization finds itself faced. The human factor, so it would seem, is given full scope by Toynbee, and in fact, he prides himself on this.

In the debate that I had with him early in 1948—a radio debate, broadcast by the B.B.C. in London—, he insisted on his belief in man's free will, in man's freedom to respond when life presented him with a challenge; and again he denied expressly that he had ever presumed to use history to tell the world's fortune. "With the awful warning of Spengler's dogmatic determinism before my eyes"—that is how he expressed it—"I have been mighty careful to treat the future of our civilization as an open question."

Of course, one can only note these asseverations with pleasure. I did so in the debate, although I could not help pointing to some features of his great work which hardly seemed to be consistent with this mental attitude. Toynbee retorted—a little impatiently this time— that he must be the last judge of what his own beliefs are. Obviously. And yet this cannot mean that we should not be at liberty to criticize the system as he has worked it out in the six volumes of his "Study of History"; and in particular, are we not entitled to ask whether his system does not, on this all-important question, come into conflict with his professed belief? I believe that it does: and if I may summarize for you the system in which Toynbee tells us he has discovered how the life of civilizations is enacted, I can point out exactly in what way the conflict occurs.

Any civilization—so he teaches us—can progress for an indefinite period, and if it breaks down, it is because of the failure of its members to respond to a challenge. The breakdown is due, in other words, to human shortcomings. Now, according to Toynbee, practically all civilizations known to history—he enumerates some thirty—have so broken down. But what does he mean by the term? It does not mean *the end,* it is only *the beginning of the end.* It opens the period of disintegration which may last for centuries. According to the system, during this disintegration period the leaders of the stricken civilization are unable to meet challenges successfully; they can at best obtain a respite, but after every crisis the situation remains, worse than it was before, and in the end, the dissolution of the broken-down civilization cannot be averted.

This is the system as Toynbee expounds it; this is the law to which, according to his theory, the life of civilizations has to conform. He explains all this so fully, he illustrates it with such an abundance of instances and cases, he returns to the leading ideas so frequently, that there is not the slightest possibility of a misunderstanding. Now I submit that it is small use telling one you are a believer in man's free will and particularly in the freedom of the human beings comprising a civilization to respond to challenges, when in fact you make an exception for this protracted period of disintegration. A number of successive generations—if we accept Toynbee's own teaching—have every now and again in history to live through these distressful circumstances. Such generations are *not* free. They struggle, but their struggles are foredoomed to failure.

There is no other end for them than catastrophe, than defeat.

There is more involved here than the question of freedom or determinism; there is an immediate connection with the subject I am discussing, the question, that is, of what Toynbee undertakes to teach us from history about the future of Western civilization. Toynbee may assure us that he has never used history to foretell the world's future, and that he looks upon the future of Western civilization as an open question. It is certainly true that he has never said in so many words that Western civilization is doomed. He has not in the "Study of History" so far dealt expressly with the prospects of our civilization— that question is reserved for some later volume. But in many passages he has referred to it, and the careful reader can be in no doubt as to his meaning. He is not perhaps quite sure, but he has the gravest apprehensions, that we are and have been ever since the late sixteenth century, in that unhappy period of disintegration in which all our efforts are in vain, in which things can only go from bad to worse, until release comes in the shape of dissolution, which at least will open the way for some new form of civilization.

This is at least what ought to be our position according to the strict tenor of the system, but now Toynbee is seen to waver. According to the system all civilizations in a period of disintegration are doomed, but now, faced with the problem of our own civilization, suddenly and most unexpectedly, he admits an exception: even if, owing to the mistakes of our ancestors, we are and have been for nearly four centuries on the downward path of disintegration, we have one possibility of reprieve. If only we would return to the faith of our fathers, be reconverted to the Christian religion, the threatening disaster might still be averted.

Professor Toynbee can always appeal to this loophole to claim that he is not a prophet of doom and, indeed, in our radio debate he did so very emphatically. If we will only give heed to his warning and follow his direction, we may still be saved. He is, however, confining our possibilities within very narrow limits, and unless we are able to accept his offer of salvation through a return to the Christian religion, the effect of his teaching must be depressing. As for me, I will own frankly that the chances of a real conversion, such as Toynbee means, appear to be so exiguous that to make the survival of our civilization depend on their being realized would almost amount to a sentence of death.

But the relative importance of religion in our civilization is itself a question on which views might differ. Assuming that religion was in a stronger position in the Middle Ages than it has been since, would it be true to say that the sense of social or international security, that the realities of justice and the opportunities for the great masses of people to lead lives capable of yielding some happiness, including even the development of spiritual values, were more firmly entrenched in the Middle Ages than they are now, in an age, which, according to Toynbee, is characterized by the corruption or the loss of faith? I doubt it very much, and I think, moreover, a very good case might be made out for the contention that problems of that kind, which most people think have to do with the health and prospects of survival of a civilization, have always been tackled, and will still have to be tackled, on a different plane from that of religion. To my way of thinking, it therefore seems the wrong policy altogether to want to concentrate attention on the issue of religion alone, and to divert it from the many other problems which have to be dealt with if we are to get safely over the troubles and difficulties which beset our civilization (difficulties which I am certainly not inclined to minimize). Toynbee, however, speaks slightingly of "our hotly canvassed and loudly advertised political and economic maladies"; for him the only really "deadly danger" is the loss of faith.

This standard of values, by the way, helps to explain his view—which at first sight will strike most people as a rather extraordinary one—that it was the wars of religion in the sixteenth century which caused the breakdown of our civilization. There have been many wars in Europe, both before and after, which were equally devastating, caused as great a loss of life, were socially no less disturbing. But that the highest good given to man, the belief in the Christian God, led to this horrible perversion of intolerance and war, that is what marks out the wars of religion for Toynbee. Their termination, too, in a system of tolerance which was merely practical and cynical, which had nothing of Christian love in it, by which absolute control over religion was vested in the secular rulers of the various national states—all that seems to him to have cut at the very foundations of our civilization. The skepticism of the succeeding period, the unbelief of a still later age, —it all flows from that terrible, from that criminal aberration. There is in this view an undeniable grandeur. It hangs logically together and is intimately connected with that estimate of the loss of religion as the really critical problem of our time.

I do not, of course, dream of denying to Toynbee the right to hold these opinions. One can differ from them, and I will just state that I do differ, that I think these views extraordinarily one-sided. To me it seems, frankly, an amazing judgment of the last three or four centuries of

European history to write them off as showing nothing but a losing fight against fate. The whole of American history is included in this sweeping verdict, for of course in his conception, America belongs organically to the sphere of Western civilization. On this point I agree wholeheartedly, but the main proposition, that our history for the last four centuries has been one of irremediable decay, becomes only the more amazing.

I just state my dissent from that main proposition without entering into any discussion. My intention is only to point out that a large view or interpretation like this one cannot possibly be proved by history, nor do I believe that it is derived from a study of history—and neither, I hasten to add, can the dissenting view be so proved or is it so derived. Both are matters of subjective conviction, and it is from this conviction that Toynbee's history is derived, not the other way round.

I have a feeling that I am stating the obvious. Yet when you read "A Study of History" you will be struck by the insistence with which the eloquent author asserts and repeats that he is conducting an empirical exploration, and that the conclusions at which he arrives, the whole system which he develops, his discovery and definition of laws by which the movement of civilizations is governed—all spring unaided from facts, facts scientifically observed and scientifically connected.

Now I contend that his conception of what an historical fact really is, of what an historical fact is worth, of what can be done with it, is open to very grave objections. Professor Toynbee does not like professional historians; he is inclined to deal somewhat contemptuously with them. Their perpetually critical attitude of mind and their eternal skepticism make him impatient. I am of course, as the French would put it, preaching for my own parish, but I can't help thinking that it is an altogether precious thing—a bracing thing that our civilization cannot do without—that the professional historian should preserve his scruples and his humility with respect to his subject, that he should be aware of the limits set to his knowledge, and that he should prefer his ignorance and his doubt to attractive but facile generalizations.

I don't mean that the historian should (as he is sometimes advised) stick to the facts. The facts are there to be used. Combinations, presentations, theories, are the important thing in history. But the historian should proceed cautiously in using the facts for these purposes. It goes without saying that he should try to ascertain the facts as exactly as possible; but the important thing is that he should remain conscious, even then, of the element of arbitrariness, of subjectivity, that necessarily enters into all combinations of facts, if only because one has to begin by selecting them; while next, one has to order them according to an idea which must, in part at least, be conceived in one's own mind.

I am quite ready to admit that academic historiography often sins by employing too much caution. This sometimes leads to a shrinking from the use of that indispensable gift of the imagination. Academic historians do not perhaps always sufficiently remember the great task of history, which is not, after all, meant to be a plaything for scholars in the seclusion of their study, but which has a great social function to fulfill. I admit all this, and up to a point I can sympathize with Toynbee's impatience. Yet I believe that the scholarly caution of which I spoke is also one of the high duties of the historian and the essential condition of his usefulness.

Toynbee, with his immense learning,

has a multitude of historical illustrations at his fingers' ends at every turn of his argument, and he discourses with never-failing brilliance and never-failing confidence on careers and personalities of statesmen or thinkers, on tendencies, movements of thought, social conditions, wars, customs of all countries and of all ages. Now the critical reader will feel that each single one of his cases might give rise to discussion. Each could be represented in a slightly or markedly different way so as no longer to substantiate his argument. They are not facts: they are subjective presentations of facts; they are combinations or interpretations of facts. As the foundations of an imposing superstructure of theory, they prove extraordinarily shifting and shaky, and this in spite of the dexterity and assurance with which Toynbee handles them.

To me it seems that all these large syntheses of history (and I include Sorokin's) are vitiated by an insufficient appreciation of the infinite complexity, of the many-sidedness, of the irreducible variety of the life of mankind in all its aspects, which is after all the stuff of which history is made. This applies with particular force when an attempt is made to establish the laws governing the cultural life of mankind.

The great Dutch historian Huizinga, who died in the last year of the war, once wrote that the height of a civilization cannot be measured. To me this seems a wise saying. It implies that civilizations cannot with any certainty be divided into higher and lower. Toynbee's rigid classification of the successive stages of one and the same civilization in a period of growth, followed after a breakdown by a period of disintegration, remains to me, after reading the many hundreds of brilliant pages in which he tries to explain and to describe it, utterly incomprehensible. To judge a civilization, or one particular stage of a civilization, steadily, and to judge it whole, is a task which I think will always be beyond the powers of the human intellect. We speak glibly—and I have done so myself and shall no doubt do so again—of a golden age, or of an age of decadence. In fact when one studies a golden age in any detail one is struck by signs of corruption or weakness or distress, at least equalling those which frighten us in our own time. On the other hand, no age of decadence in history is without the redeeming features of effort or of new birth. But to measure the one set of factors against the other is what the historian can never do with any certainty.

It is sometimes thought that we are beset by these difficulties only when facing the mystery of our own time. The historian has before him something that is completed, something that can be turned around and around on the dissecting table. What can help him in his analysis to reach a final verdict, so it is imagined, is that he knows the outcome. Surely that must be a sufficient indication of the trend of the period he is studying? No doubt the historian is often guided by the outcome in his judgments, and he cannot neglect the evidence of the outcome. But to think that it will solve all his riddles for him is to fall into a very dangerous delusion. The factors by which the outcome was brought about are numerous, and they are again dissimilar. How shall one decide whether it was the purely spiritual, or the purely material factors that were decisive? One can guess, one can have one's personal conviction; one cannot prove.

Toynbee, no doubt, tries to simplify the problem by contending that the life of a civilization is completely self-reliant, that its fate is governed by spiritual forces alone. I am far from being an adherent of historic materialism, but this exclusive spiritualism is more than I can swallow.

Toynbee tries to prove elaborately, for instance, that no civilization has ever been broken down by outside violence. It is always by the spiritual shortcomings of the civilization itself that the breakdown is brought about. The argument is ingenious, but utterly unconvincing. If the thesis were true, the problem for the historian would still be staggering in its complexity, but it would be simplified. If one has to reject the thesis, as I do reject it, one can say only the more positively that the historian cannot fix the past in an unshakable pattern that will be valid for everyone, and from which conclusions as to the future can be drawn.

I need not, I trust, explain that I am not arguing against history as being of no use for the present. I believe, with Burckhardt, that, although it does not yield lessons for the immediate occasion, its study can make us wiser. And let me say that by *us* I do not mean the professional historians particularly; I mean the community in whose midst history is constantly being made. I believe in the great indispensable value of historical insight for civilized society. But we must not expect of history what history cannot possibly give—certainty. I quarrel with Toynbee not when he soars above the ground of history where we others plod: the spectacle enthralls me even when I remain unconvinced; I admire the sweep of his imagination; I feel warmed by the glow of his enthusiasm, I am ready to regard his confessions of faith as significant manifestations in the struggle of minds that constitutes the cultural life of our time. But I enter my *caveat*[1] when the great work is presented to the public as a work of scientific thought. As a prophet, as a poet, Toynbee is remarkable, and nobody will grudge him his appeals to history: one can only feel the liveliest admiration for his historical knowledge and for the inexhaustible picturesqueness and ingenuity with which he draws upon it. But when he pretends to be conducting a severely logical argument and builds up a system in so many stages and parts supposed to be based on a strictly empirical investigation, then I feel I must demur. And the more so, as it all leads to a conclusion which seems to me a dangerous one. Be converted or perish, Toynbee tells us; and he says it as if speaking with the authority of history behind him. But history does not warrant any such dilemma. Only the mystic will read into it the promise of a mystical salvation. To the rest of us it does not convey a message of despair.

_____

[1] "Let the reader beware"—Ed.

Born in Russia and exiled by revolution and civil war in 1922, PITIRIM A. SOROKIN (1889–1968) described his Doctor Zhivago–like life in *A Long Journey* (1963). During World War I, Sorokin prepared himself for a professorship in criminal law, but the upheavals of his time destined him for sociology. In 1919–1920 Sorokin helped to organize a sociology department at the University of Leningrad; in 1930–1931, he opened one at Harvard where he also founded the Research Center for Creative Altruism (1945). After his major work *Social and Cultural Dynamics* (1937–1941) Sorokin never tired of analyzing social philosophies of an age of crisis in books and articles. Here, he criticizes a pattern of the past which he himself is supposed to have supported.*

Pitirim A. Sorokin

Lasting and Dying Factors in the World's Cultures

The scholars in question[1] made two fundamental errors in their theories: first, they confused organized social groups or inhabited areas with unified cultures or civilizations; second, they chose for their "civilizations" social groups of different kinds, thus committing the error of uniting in one logical class, groups of different character and giving them the same name. Indeed, their very classification of civilizations . . . , whether Egyptian, Sumeric, Jewish, Arabic, Iranian, Hindu, Chinese, or Greek, is actually a classification of social groups or even of certain vast inhabited areas— not of systems of culture or civilization.

[1] Danilevsky, Spengler, and Toynbee—Ed.

This error is aggravated by an additional mistake: even as a classification of social groups or inhabited areas it is inconsistent in that it puts into a single class "civilization" groups and areas of very diverse character. Some of their "civilizations" are really *language* groups (the totality of persons having the same native language and many similar cultural traits). Others are *state* groups; *religious* groups; *locality,* or *territorial* groups; or more *complex* groups, such as the totality of individuals sharing the same state, territory, language, and religion. Such a "civilization" as that of Greece is primarily a *language* group; for Greece as a whole has hardly ever been united into a single state. Such "civilizations" as those of

Sparta, the Ottoman Empire, and Rome are essentially *state* groups. The Spartans differed from other Greeks not in respect to language but through belonging to an independent state. The Ottoman "civilization" is the Ottoman empire group, made of a multitude of different language groups never amalgamated into one nation or one language or religious group. "Civilizations" like those of the Buddhistic Chinese, the Mohammedans, the Hindus, or the Near Eastern Christians are mainly *religious* or *territorial* groups. The Chinese, Iranian, and Russian "civilizatons" represent essentially complex groups—the totality of individuals belonging to the same state and territory and having the same language. Finally, a "civilization" like the Hellenistic (in so far as it was a phase of Greco Roman "civilization") does not represent even an organized group: the term is merely a name covering a multitude of different groups not united by a common state, a common language, a common religion, or any other common cultural or civilizational trait.

Such is the curious assortment of heterogeneous social groups and areas covered by the same name, assigned to the same class of "civilization," and fused into an "organic unity." Logically this procedure is as sound as that of a biologist who puts into the same class—that of "mammals"—a lion, a bird, a fish, an ant, and an area of New England! The procedure explains, however, how and why Danilevsky, Spengler, and Toynbee reached their conclusion respecting the death of civilizazations. The *longevity, or life span, of almost all organized groups is finite.* According to the nature of the group, it varies from a few moments to a few years, decades, or centuries—in rare cases, a few thousands of years. Thus the average life span of contemporary small economic organiza-

tions is about three years; that of bigger business firms about six years; and that of the large business concerns about twenty-eight years. Small local cultural groups survive, on an average, about two or three years. The longevity of the family ranges from a few days or years to some three hundred years, rarely exceeding this duration, a longevity of from one to three generations being modal. Seventy-seven per cent of the existing universities and colleges were founded after 1800, very few, if any, antedating the twelfth century. Of existing cities with a population of 100,000 or over, approximately 40 per cent emerged after 1600, 21 per cent were founded between the eleventh and the fifteenth centuries, and only 18 per cent antedate the fifth century A.D. The life span of contemporary small cities is considerably shorter. The duration of states varies from a few years up to two thousand years or over, most of the existing states (36) having an age of approximately one hundred years or less. Small religious groups disappear within a few years or decades. The life span of major religions, such as Hinduism, Taoism, Confucianism, Buddhism, Jainism, Judaism, Christianity, and Mohammedanism, has ranged from approximately 1,300 years up to 3,500 years or over. Similarly, many small language groups have had a life span of only a few decades. Larger ones have existed for several centuries; a few, for one or two thousand years.

All in all, most social groups rarely survive for more than a few centuries. Virtually all organized groups—the state, the family, the language group, the political party, even the religious group—are mortal: after a time they disintegrate and dissolve as social individualities, though this dissolution does not mean either the death of their members or the disappearance of their total culture or civilization.

While the group may dissolve, all or a considerable part of its total culture or civilization may be—and usually is—taken over by other groups, and often expanded and enriched by them. Although the Greek states were dissolved, yet Greek culture or civilization has been appropriated, in its greater part, by many other groups and has spread far beyond the confines of Greece and the Hellenic world. The same is true of practically any other great culture that has possessed vital values.

Danilevsky, Spengler, and Toynbee, having mistaken a motley assortment of social groups for civilization, and having observed that social groups are mortal, rashly concluded that both ordinary and major cultures and civilizations die *in toto*. The states of ancient Egypt, Sumeria, Babylonia, and Rome are extinct; so also are many past language, religious, and territorial groups. Nevertheless, a great deal of the total culture or civilization of these groups is still functioning in the contemporary sociocultural world either in its original form or in a disguised and modified form as a part and parcel of our living "civilization." The scientific discoveries of earlier civilizations; their philosophical systems; their religious systems; their law, ethics, language, literature, architecture, music, painting, sculpture, and drama; their forms of political, economic, and social organization; their manners and mores—these elements make up the lion's share of today's living civilization. If, indeed, we were to subtract from our Western civilization all the values inherited from the "dead civilizations," particularly those of the Greco-Roman and the Jewish world (including Christianity), the remainder would be unbelievably meager and paltry, as well as incoherent.

To sum up: Whichever of the foregoing meanings of the term "death of civilization" we take, the formulas of the "undertakers of civilization" appear to be essentially untenable.

The basic fallacy of the main premises of Danilevsky, Spengler, and Toynbee vitiates also many other conclusions of these authors, such as the inference that all great civilizations pass through a similar life cycle of childhood, maturity, and old age, or of spring, summer, autumn (including the "Indian summer"), and winter; that each is based, throughout its whole life process, upon one specific idea or value, the Hindu civilization being regarded as religious; the Greek, as artistic; the Western, as scientific; and so on. Nevertheless, their works contain many sound, valuable, and even profound ideas, the analysis of which is beyond the scope of this paper.

ARNOLD J. TOYNBEE (b. 1889) began his academic
career as tutor at Balliol College in Oxford. After
World War I, he worked on *A Survey of International
Affairs* (1920–1946), served as member of the British
peace delegation in Paris 1919 and 1946, and was a
professor at London University. *A Study of History*
(1934–1961) made him the popular symbol of the
universal historian in our time. In this lecture to
American students Toynbee corrects the impression
he made on P. Geyl, namely, that his pattern of the
past was inescapably repetitive and unnecessarily
pessimistic.*

Arnold J. Toynbee

Does History Repeat Itself?

Does history repeat itself? In our Western world in the eighteenth and nineteenth centuries, this question used to be debated as an academic exercise. The spell of well-being which our civilization was enjoying at the time had dazzled our grandfathers into the quaint pharisaical notion that they were "not as other men are"; they had come to believe that our Western society was exempt from the possibility of falling into those mistakes and mishaps that have been the ruin of certain other civilizations whose history, from beginning to end, is an open book. To us, in our generation, the old question has rather suddenly taken on a new and very practical significance. We have awakened to the truth (how, one wonders, could we ever have been blind to it?) that Western man and his works are no more invulnerable than the now extinct civilizations of the Aztecs and the Incas, the Sumerians and the Hittites. So to-day, with some anxiety, we are searching the scriptures of the past to find out whether they contain a lesson that we can decipher. Does history give us any information about our own prospects? And, if it does, what is the burden of it? Does it spell out for us an inexorable doom, which we can merely await with folded hands—resigning ourselves, as best we may, to a fate that we cannot avert or even modify by our own efforts? Or does it inform us, not of certainties, but of probabilities, or bare possibilities, in our own future? The practical difference is vast, for, on this second alternative, so far from being stunned

*From *Civilization on Trial* by Arnold J. Toynbee. Copyright 1948 by Oxford University Press, Inc. Reprinted by permission. Pp. 29–38.

into passivity, we should be roused to action. On this second alternative, the lesson of history would not be like an astrologer's horoscope; it would be like a navigator's chart, which affords the seafarer who has the intelligence to use it a much greater hope of avoiding shipwreck than when he was sailing blind, because it gives him the means, if he has the skill and courage to use them, of steering a course between charted rocks and reefs.

It will be seen that our question needs defining before we plunge into an attempt to answer it. When we ask ourselves "Does history repeat itself?" do we mean no more than "Does history turn out to have repeated itself, on occasions, in the past?" Or are we asking whether history is governed by inviolable laws which have not only taken effect in every past case to which they have applied but are also bound to take effect in every similar situation that may arise in the future? On this second interpretation, the word "does" would mean "must"; on the other interpretation it would mean "may." On this issue, the writer of the present article may as well put his cards on the table at once. He is not a determinist in his reading of the riddle of human life. He believes that where there is life there is hope, and that, with God's help, man is master of his own destiny, at least to some extent in some respects.

But as soon as we have taken our stand on this issue between freedom and necessity that is raised by the ambiguous word "does," we find ourselves called upon to define what we mean by the word "history." If we have to limit the field of history to events that are wholly within the control of human wills, then, to be sure, for a non-determinist no difficulty would arise. But do such events ever actually occur in real life? In our personal experi-

ence, when we are making a decision, do we not always find ourselves only partly free and partly bound by past events and present facts in our own life and in our social and physical environment? Is not history itself, in the last analysis, a vision of the whole universe on the move in the four-dimensional framework of space-time? And, in this all-embracing panorama, are there not many events that the most staunch believer in the freedom of the human will would admit, as readily as the most thorough-going determinist, to be inexorably recurrent and precisely predictable?

Some events of this undisputedly recurrent predictable order may have little apparent bearing upon human affairs—as, for example, the repetitions of history in nebulae outside the system of the Milky Way. There are, however, some very obvious cyclic movements in physical nature that do affect human affairs in the most intimate fashion—as, for example, the recurrent predictable alternations of day and night and of the seasons of the year. The day-and-night cycle governs all human work; it dictates the schedules of the transportation systems of our cities, sets the times of their rush hours, and weighs on the minds of the commuters whom it shuttles to and fro, twice in every twenty-four hours, between "dormitory" and "workshop." The cycle of the seasons governs human life itself by governing our food supply.

It is true that man, by taking thought, can win a measure of freedom from these physical cycles that is beyond the reach of birds and beasts. Though the individual cannot break the tyranny of the day-and-night cycle by leading a waking life for twenty-four hours in the day, like the legendary Egyptian Pharaoh Mycerinus, human society can achieve Mycerinus' mythical feat collectively by a planned co-operation and a division of labour. Industrial plants can be operated for twenty-four hours in the day by successive shifts of workers, and the labours of workers who work by day can be prepared for and be followed up by the labours of other workers who rest by day and work by night. The tyranny of the seasons, again, has been broken by a Western society that has expanded from the northern temperate zone into the tropics and the southern temperate zone and has devised a technique of refrigeration. Nevertheless, these triumphs of man's mind and will over the tyranny of the two physical cycles of the day and the year are comparatively small gains for human freedom, remarkable though these triumphs are. On the whole, these recurrent predictable events in physical nature remain masters of human life—even at the present level of Western man's technology—and they show their mastery by subduing human affairs, as far as their empire over them extends, to their own recurrent predictable pattern.

But there are, perhaps, human acts, in other fields of action, that are not—or, at any rate not so completely—under physical nature's control? Let us examine this question in a familiar concrete case. When, in the last days of April 1865, the horses that, in the first days of that month, had been the cavalry and artillery horses of the Army of Northern Virginia, were being driven behind the plough by the men who, at the beginning of that April, had been General Lee's cavalrymen and artillerymen, those men and horses were once again performing an annually recurrent agricultural operation which they themselves had performed a number of times before in their lives and which predecessors of theirs, in the Old World

before Europeans discovered the New World, and in other societies before our Western society's birth, had been performing, year by year, for some five or six thousand years past. The invention of ploughing is coeval with the species of society that we call civilizations, and pre-plough methods of agriculture—likewise governed by the year cycle—were already in use for perhaps an equal length of time before that, during the neolithic dawn by which the sunrise of civilization was heralded. In the spring of 1865, agriculture in the ex-Confederate States of North America was governed by the seasons very rigidly. A few weeks' delay, and the season would have been too late—with the disastrous consequence that the food-producing capacities of those horses and men would have been lost to the community for a whole year longer.

Thus, in the last days of April 1865, the horses and men of the former Army of Northern Virginia were performing a historical act—the spring ploughing—which had repeated itself, by that date, some five or six thousand times at least, and was still repeating itself in 1947. (In that year the writer of this article witnessed the spring ploughing in Kentucky, and noted the farmers' anxiety when, in the middle of that April, their work was interrupted by heavy rainfall.)

But what about the history that General Lee's horses and men were making, not at the end of April, but at the beginning? Is the kind of history that is represented by the last act of the Civil War a kind that repeats itself—as ploughing and commuting repeat themselves owing to their close and obvious dependence on recurrent predictable cycles in physical nature? Are we not confronted here with a kind of human action that is more or less independent of physical cycles and is capable of overriding them? Suppose that General Lee had not found himself constrained to capitulate till June 1865? Or suppose that, General Lee having capitulated when he did, General Grant had not been moved to make his celebrated concession of allowing the Confederate soldiers who had just laid down their arms to take their horses back with them to their farms, notwithstanding the contrary provision in the terms of surrender that had just been agreed upon. Would not either of these hypothetical man-made variations on the actual course of historical events have prevented history from repeating itself in the Southern States in the spring ploughing of 1865?

The province of history that we are considering now is one that used to be treated as the whole field of history before the provinces of economic and social history were opened up. In this old-fashioned field of battles and policies, captains and kings, does history turn out to have repeated itself as it does in fields of human activity that are manifestly governed by cycles in the movement of physical nature? Was the Civil War, for instance, a unique event, or do we find other historical events that display sufficient similarity and affinity to it to warrant us in treating it and them as so many representatives of a class of events in which history has repeated itself at least to some extent? The present writer inclines to this latter view.

The crisis represented in American history by the Civil War was, surely, repeated in a significant sense in the contemporary crisis in German history that is represented by the Bismarckian wars of 1864–71. In both cases, an imperfect political union had threatened to dissolve altogether. In both cases, the issue between the dissolution of the union and its effective establishment was decided by war. In both cases, the partisans of effective union won, and, in both, one of the causes of their victory was their technological and industrial superiority over their opponents. In both, finally, the victory of the cause of union was followed by a great industrial expansion which turned both the post-bellum United States and the Second German Reich into formidable industrial competitors of Great Britain. And here we have hit upon another repetition of history; for, throughout the century ending about 1870, the industrial revolution in Great Britain might have appeared to be a unique historical event, whereas, since 1870, it has come to appear, in its true light, as simply the earliest instance of an economic transformation which was eventually to occur likewise in a number of other Western countries and in some non-Western countries too. Moreover, if we shift our attention from the economic common feature of industrialization to the political common feature of federal union, we shall see the history of the United States and Germany at this point repeating itself once again in the history of a third country—in this case not Great Britain but Canada, whose constituent provinces entered into their present federation in 1867, two years after the *de facto* re-establishment of the unity of the United States in 1865 and four years before the foundation of the Second German Reich in 1871.

In the formation, in the modern Western world, of a number of federal unions, and in the industrialization of these and other countries, we see history repeating itself in the sense of producing a number of more or less contemporary examples of the same human achievement. The contemporaneity of the different instances is, however, no more than approximate.

The industrial revolution occurred as an apparently unique event in Great Britain at least two generations before its occurrence in America, and Germany proved it to be a repetitive phenomenon. The insecurely welded pre-Civil-War United States had existed for "four score and seven years," and the ramshackle post-Napoleonic German Confederation for half a century, before the crucial events of the eighteen-sixties proved that federal union was a repetitive pattern which was to recur not only in Canada but in Australia, South Africa, and Brazil. Contemporaneity is not an essential condition for the repetition of history on the political and cultural plane of human affairs. The historical events that repeat themselves may be strictly contemporary or they may overlap in time or they may be entirely non-contemporaneous with one another.

The picture remains the same when we turn to the consideration of the greatest human institutions and experiences that are known to us: the civilizations in their births and growths, their breakdowns, declines, and falls; the higher religions in their foundation and evolution. Measured by our subjective personal measuring rod of the average span of the memory of a single human being who lives to a normal old age, the time interval that divides our present generation from the date of the emergence of the Sumerian civilization in the fourth millennium B.C. or from the date of the beginning of the Christian era itself seems, no doubt, a very long one. Yet it is infinitesimally small on the objective time scale that has recently been given to us by the discoveries of our geologists and astronomers. Our modern Western physical science tells us that the human race has been in existence on this planet for at least 600,000

and perhaps a million years, life for at least 500 million and perhaps 800 million years, and the planet itself for possibly 2000 million years. On this time scale the last five or six thousand years that have seen the births of civilizations, and the last three or four thousand years that have seen the births of higher religions are periods of such infinitesimal brevity that it would be impossible to show them, drawn to scale, on any chart of the whole history of this planet up to date. On this true time scale, these events of "ancient history" are virtually contemporary with our own lifetime, however remote they may appear to be when viewed through the magnifying lens of the individual human midget's subjective mental vision.

The conclusion seems to be that human history does turn out, on occasions, to have repeated itself up to date in a significant sense even in spheres of human activity in which the human will is at its nearest to being master of the situation and is least under the domination of cycles in physical nature. Must we go on to conclude that, after all, the determinists are right and that what looks like free will is an illusion? In the present writer's opinion, the correct conclusion is just the opposite. As he sees it, this tendency towards repetition, which thus asserts itself in human affairs, is an instance of one of the well-known devices of the creative faculty. The works of creation are apt to occur in bunches: a bunch of representatives of a species, a bunch of species of a genus. And the value of such repetitions is, after all, not difficult to discern. Creation could hardly make any headway at all if each new form of creature were not represented by numerous eggs distributed among numerous baskets. How else could a creator, human or divine, provide himself with sufficient materials for bold and fruitful experiment and with effective means of retrieving inevitable failures? If human history repeats itself, it does so in accordance with the general rhythm of the universe; but the significance of this pattern of repetition lies in the scope that it gives for the work of creation to go forward. In this light, the repetitive element in history reveals itself as an instrument for freedom of creative action, and not as an indication that God and man are the slaves of fate. . . .

According to Webster's dictionary physiognomy is "the practice of trying to judge character and mental qualities by observation of bodily, especially facial, features." OSWALD SPENGLER tried to grasp the "soul" of a culture and the "state of mind" of a civilization by the observation of their external characteristics. Because to Spengler world history meant city history, the best illustration of his physiognomic approach is perhaps this sketch of the city's changing image as it goes through the revolving door of cultural growth and civilizational decay.*

Oswald Spengler

The Soul of the City

It is, above all, the expression of the city's "visage" that has a history. The play of this facial expression, indeed, is almost the spiritual history of the Culture itself. First we have the little proto-cities of the Gothic and other Early Cultures, which almost efface themselves in the landscape, which are still genuine peasant-houses crowded under the shadow of a stronghold or a sanctuary, and without inward change become town-houses merely in the sense that they have neighbour-houses instead of fields and meadows around them. The peoples of the Early Culture gradually became town-peoples, and accordingly there are not only specifically Chinese, Indian, Apollinian, and Faustian town-forms, but, moreover, Armenian and Syrian, Ionian and Etruscan, German and French and English town-physiognomies. There is a city of Phidias, a city of Rembrandt, a city of Luther. These designations, and the mere names of Granada, Venice, and Nürnberg conjure up at once quite definite images, for all that the Culture produces in religion, art, and knowledge has been produced in such cities. While it was still the spirit of knights' castles and rural monasteries that evoked the Crusades, the Reformation is urban and belongs to narrow streets and steep-gabled houses. The great Epic, which speaks and sings of the blood, belongs to *Pfalz* [palace] and *Burg* [castle], but the Drama, in which *awakened* life tests itself, is city-poetry, and the great

*From *The Decline of the West,* Vol. II, by Oswald Spengler, trans. by Charles Francis Atkinson. Copyright 1928 and renewed 1956 by Alfred A. Knopf, Inc. Reprinted by permission of the publisher. Pp. 93–94, 96–100, and 102–105. This is published in Britain by Allen & Unwin Ltd.

Novel, the survey of all things human by the *emancipated* intellect, presupposes the world-city. Apart from really genuine folk-song, the only lyrism is of the city. Apart from the "eternal" peasant-art, there is only urban painting and architecture, with a swift and soon-ended history.

And these stone visages that have incorporated in their light-world the humanness of the citizen himself and, like him, are all eye and intellect—how distinct the language of form that they talk, how different from the rustic drawl of the landscape! The silhouette of the great city, its roofs and chimneys, the towers and domes on the horizon! What a language is imparted to us through *one* look at Nürnberg or Florence, Damascus or Moscow, Peking or Benares. What do we know of the Classical cities, seeing that we do not know the lines that they presented under the Southern noon, under clouds in the morning, in the starry night? The courses of the streets, straight or crooked, broad or narrow; the houses, low or tall, bright or dark, that in all Western cities turn their façades, *their faces,* and in all Eastern cities turn their backs, blank wall and railing, towards the street; the spirit of squares and corners, impasses and prospects, fountains and monuments, churches or temples or mosques, amphitheatres and railway stations, bazaars and town-halls! The suburbs, too, of neat garden-villas or of jumbled blocks of flats, rubbish-heaps and allotments; the fashionable quarter and the slum area, the Subura of Classical Rome and the Faubourg Saint-Germain of Paris, ancient Baiae and modern Nice, the little town-picture like Bruges and Rothenburg and the sea of houses like Babylon, Tenochtitlan, Rome, and London! All this has history and *is* history. One major political event—and the visage of the town falls into different folds. Napoleon gave to Bourbon Paris, Bismarck gave to worthy little Berlin, a new mien. But the Country stands by, uninfluenced, suspicious and irritated. . . .

The peasant is the eternal man, independent of every Culture that ensconces itself in the cities. He precedes it, he outlives it, a dumb creature propagating himself from generation to generation, limited to soil-bound callings and aptitudes, a mystical soul, a dry, shrewd understanding that sticks to practical matters, the origin and the ever-flowing source of the blood that makes world-history in the cities.

Whatever the Culture up there in the city conceives in the way of stateforms, economic customs, articles of faith, implements, knowledge, art, he receives mistrustfully and hesitatingly; though in the end he may accept these things, never is he altered in kind thereby. Thus the West-European peasant outwardly took in all the dogmas of the Councils from the great Lateran to that of Trent, just as he took in the products of mechanical engineering and those of the French Revolution—but he remains what he was, what he already was in Charlemagne's day. The present-day piety of the peasant is older than Christianity; his gods are more ancient than those of any higher religion. Remove from him the pressure of the great cities and he will revert to the state of nature without feeling that he is losing anything. His real ethic, his real metaphysic, which no scholar of the city has yet thought it worth while to discover, lie outside all religious and spiritual history, have in fact no history at all.

The city is intellect. The Megalopolis is "free" intellect. It is in resistance to the "feudal" powers of blood and tradition that the burgherdom or bourgeoisie, the intellectual class, begins to be conscious of its own separate existence. It upsets thrones and limits old rights in the name of reason and above all in the name of "the People," which henceforward means exclusively the people of the city. Democracy is the political form in which the townsman's outlook upon the world is demanded of the peasantry also. The urban intellect reforms the great religion of the springtime and sets up by the side of the old religion of noble and priest, the new religion of the Tiers État, *liberal science.* The city assumes the lead and control of economic history in replacing the primitive values of the land, which are for ever inseparable from the life and thought of the rustic, by the *absolute idea of money* as distinct from goods. The immemorial country word for exchange of goods is "barter"; even when one of the things exchanged is precious metal, the underlying idea of the process is not yet *monetary*—i.e., it does not involve the abstraction of value from things and its fixation in metallic or fictitious quantities intended to *measure* things qua "commodities." Caravan expeditions and Viking voyages in the springtime are made between land-settlements and imply barter or booty, whereas in the Late period they are made between cities and mean "money." This is the distinction between the Normans before and the Hansa and Venetians after the Crusades, and between the seafarers of Mycenaean times and those of the later colonization period in Greece. The City means not only intellect, but also money.

Presently there arrived an epoch when the development of the city had reached such a point of power that it had no longer to defend itself against country and chivalry, but on the contrary had become a despotism against which the land and its basic orders of society were fighting a hopeless defensive battle—in the spiritual domain against nationalism, in the polit-ical against democracy, in the economic against money. At this period the number of cities that really counted as historically dominant had already become very small. And with this there arose the profound distinction—which was above all a spiritual distinction—between the great city and the little city or town. The latter, very significantly called the country-town, was a part of the no longer co-efficient countryside. It was not that the difference between townsman and rustic had become lessened in such towns, but that this difference had become negligible as compared with the new difference between them and the great city. The sly-shrewdness of the country and the intelligence of the megalopolis are two forms of waking-consciousness between which reciprocal understanding is scarcely possible. Here again it is evident that what counts is not the number of inhabitants, but the spirit. It is evident, moreover, that in all great cities nooks remained in which relics of an almost rural mankind lived in their byeways much as if they were on the land, and the people on the two sides of the street were almost in the relation of two villages. In fact, a pyramid of mounting civism, of decreasing number and increasing field of view, leads up from such quasi-rural elements, in ever-narrowing layers, to the small number of genuine megalopolitans at the top, who are at home wherever their spiritual postulates are satisfied.

With this the notion of money attains to full abstractness. It no longer merely *serves* for the understanding of economic intercourse, but *subjects* the exchange of goods to *its own* evolution. It values things, no longer as between each other, but *with reference to itself.* Its relation to the soil and to the man of the soil has so completely vanished, that in the economic thought of the leading cities—the "money-markets"—it is ignored. Money has now become a power, and, moreover, a power that is wholly intellectual and merely figured in the metal it uses, a power the reality of which resides in the waking-consciousness of the upper stratum of an economically active population, a power that makes those concerned with it just as dependent upon itself as the peasant was dependent upon the soil. There is monetary thought, just as there is mathematical or juristic.

But the earth is actual and natural, and money is abstract and artificial, a mere "category"—like "virtue" in the imagination of the Age of Enlightenment. And therefore every primary, pre-civic economy is dependent upon and held in bondage by the cosmic powers, the soil, the climate, the type of man, whereas money, as the pure form of economic intercourse within the waking-consciousness, is no more limited in potential scope by actuality than are the quantities of the mathematical and the logical world. Just as no view of facts hinders us from constructing as many non-Euclidean geometries as we please, so in the developed megalopolitan economics there is no longer any inherent objection to increasing "money" or to thinking, so to say, in other money-dimensions. This has nothing to do with the availability of gold or with any values in actuality at all. There is no standard and no sort of goods in which the value of the talent in the Persian Wars can be compared with its value in the Egyptian booty of Pompey. Money has become, for man as an economic animal, a form of the activity of waking-consciousness, having no longer any roots in Being. This is the basis of its monstrous power over every beginning Civilization, which is always an unconditional *dictatorship of money,* though taking different forms in different

Cultures. But this is the reason, too, for the want of solidity, which eventually leads to its losing its power and its meaning, so that at the last, as in Diocletian's time, it disappears from the thought of the closing Civilization, and the primary values of the soil return anew to take its place.

Finally, there arises the monstrous symbol and vessel of the completely emancipated intellect, the world-city, the centre in which the course of a world-history ends by winding itself up. A handful of gigantic places in each Civilization disfranchises and disvalues the entire motherland of its own Culture under the contemptuous name of "the provinces." The "provinces" are now everything whatsoever—land, town, *and* city—except these two or three points. There are no longer noblesse and bourgeoisie, freemen and slaves, Hellenes and Barbarians, believers and unbelievers, *but only cosmopolitans and provincials.* All other contrasts pale before this one, which dominates all events, all habits of life, all views of the world. . . .

These final cities are *wholly* intellect. Their houses are no longer, as those of the Ionic and the Baroque were, derivatives of the old peasant's house, whence the Culture took its spring into history. They are, generally speaking, no longer houses in which Vesta and Janus, Lares and Penates, have any sort of footing, but mere premises which have been fashioned, not by blood but by requirements, not by feeling but by the spirit of commercial enterprise. So long as the hearth has a pious meaning as the actual and genuine centre of a family, the old relation to the land is not wholly extinct. But when *that,* too, follows the rest into oblivion, and the mass of tenants and bed-occupiers in the sea of houses leads a vagrant existence from shelter to shelter like the hunters and pastors of the "pre-" time, then the intellectual nomad is completely developed. This city is a world, is *the* world. Only as a whole, as a human dwelling-place, has it meaning, the houses being merely the stones of which it is assembled. . . .

But no wretchedness, no compulsion, not even a clear vision of the madness of this development, avails to neutralize the attractive force of these daemonic creations. The wheel of Destiny rolls on to its end; the birth of the City entails its death. Beginning and end, a peasant cottage and a tenement-block are related to one another as soul and intellect, as blood and stone. But "Time" is no abstract phrase, but a name for the actuality of Irreversibility. Here there is only forward, never back. Long, long ago the country bore the country-town and nourished it with her best blood. Now the giant city sucks the country dry, insatiably and incessantly demanding and devouring fresh streams of men, till it wearies and dies in the midst of an almost uninhabited waste of country. Once the full sinful beauty of this last marvel of all history has captured a victim, it never lets him go. Primitive folk can loose themselves from the soil and wander, but the intellectual nomad never. Homesickness for the great city is keener than any other nostalgia. Home is for him any one of these giant cities, but even the nearest village is alien territory. He would sooner die upon the pavement than go "back" to the land. Even disgust at this pretentiousness, weariness of the thousand-hued glitter, the *taedium vitae* that in the end overcomes many, does not set them free. They take the City with them into the mountains or on the sea. They have lost the country within themselves and will never regain it outside.

What makes the man of the world-cities incapable of living on any but this artificial footing is that the cosmic beat in his being is ever decreasing, while the tensions of his waking-consciousness become more and more dangerous. It must be remembered that in a microcosm the animal, waking side supervenes upon the vegetable side, that of being, and not vice versa. Beat and tension, blood and intellect, Destiny and Causality are to one another as the country-side in bloom is to the city of stone, as something existing *per se* to something existing dependently. Tension without cosmic pulsation to animate it is the transition to nothingness. But Civilization is nothing but tension. The head, in all the outstanding men of the Civilizations, is dominated exclusively by an expression of extreme tension. Intelligence is only the capacity for understanding at high tension, and in every Culture these heads are the types of its final men—one has only to compare them with the peasant heads, when such happen to emerge in the swirl of the great city's street-life. The advance, too, from peasant wisdom—"slimness," mother wit, instinct, based as in other animals upon the sensed beat of life—through the city-spirit to the cosmopolitan intelligence—the very word with its sharp ring betraying the disappearance of the old cosmic foundation—can be described as a steady diminution of the Destiny-feeling and an unrestrained augmentation of needs according to the operation of a Causality. Intelligence is the replacement of unconscious living by exercise in thought, masterly, but bloodless and jejune. The intelligent visage is similar in all races —what is recessive in them is, precisely, race. The weaker the feeling for the necessity and self-evidence of Being, the more the habit of "elucidation" grows, the more the fear in the waking-consciousness comes to be stilled by causal methods.

Hence the assimilation of knowledge with demonstrability, and the substitution of scientific theory, the causal myth, for the religious. Hence, too, money-in-the-abstract as the pure causality of economic life, in contrast to rustic barter, which is pulsation and not a system of tensions.

Tension, when it has become intellectual, knows no form of recreation but that which is specific to the world-city—namely, *détente,* relaxation, distraction. Genuine play, *joie de vivre,* pleasure, inebriation, are products of the cosmic beat and as such no longer comprehensible in their essence. But the relief of hard, intensive brain-work by its opposite—conscious and practised fooling—of intellectual tension by the bodily tension of sport, of bodily tension by the sensual straining after "pleasure" and the spiritual straining after the "excitements" of betting and competitions, of the pure logic of the day's work by a consciously enjoyed mysticism—all this is common to the world-cities of all the Civilizations. Cinema, Expressionism, Theosophy, boxing contests, nigger[1] dances, poker, and racing—one can find it all in Rome. Indeed, the connoisseur might extend his researches to the Indian, Chinese, and Arabian world-cities as well. To name but one example, if one reads the Kamasutram one understands how it was that Buddhism *also* appealed to men's tastes, and then the bullfighting scenes in the Palace of Cnossus will be looked at with quite different eyes. A cult, no doubt, underlay them, but there was a savour over it all, as over Rome's fashionable

---

[1] At the time this was written, the word designated the type of tap dancing which together with the jazz band swept the cities of Europe in the roaring twenties and had perhaps even a positive, if patronizing, connotation. The neutral term "Negro" would have denoted the native folk dances of Africa and not the popular export from the American South—Ed.

Isis-cult in the neighbourhood of the Circus Maximus.

And then when Being is sufficiently uprooted and Waking-Being sufficiently strained, there suddenly emerges into the bright light of history a phenomenon that has long been preparing itself underground and now steps forward to make an end of the drama—the *sterility of civilized man.* This is not something that can be grasped as a plain matter of Causality (as modern science naturally enough has tried to grasp it); it is to be understood as an essentially *metaphysical* turn towards death. The last man of the world-city no longer *wants* to live—he may cling to life as an individual, but as a type, as an aggregate, no, for it is a characteristic of this collective existence that it eliminates the terror of death. That which strikes the true peasant with a deep and inexplicable fear, the notion that the family and the name may be extinguished, has now lost its meaning. The continuance of the blood-relation in the visible world is no longer a duty of the blood, and the destiny of being the last of the line is no longer felt as a doom. Children do not happen, not because children have become impossible, but principally because intelligence at the peak of intensity can no longer find any reason for their existence. Let the reader try to merge himself in the soul of the peasant. He has sat on his glebe from primeval times, or has fastened his clutch in it, to adhere to it with his blood. He is rooted in it as the descendant of his forbears and as the forbear of future descendants. *His* house, *his* property, means, here, not the temporary connexion of person and thing for a brief span of years, but an enduring and inward union of *eternal* land and *eternal* blood. It is only from this mystical conviction of settlement that the great epochs of the cycle—procreation, birth, and death—derive that metaphysical element of wonder which condenses in the symbolism of custom and religion that all landbound people possess. For the "last men" all this is past and gone. Intelligence and sterility are allied in old families, old peoples, and old Cultures, not merely because in each microcosm the overstrained and fettered animal-element is eating up the plant element, but also because the waking-consciousness assumes that being is normally regulated by causality. That which the man of intelligence, most significantly and characteristically, labels as "natural impulse" or "life-force," he not only knows, but also values, causally, giving it the place amongst his other needs that his judgment assigns to it. When the ordinary thought of a highly cultivated people begins to regard "having children" as a question of *pro's* and *con's,* the great turning-point has come. For Nature knows nothing of *pro* and *con.* Everywhere, wherever life is actual, reigns an inward organic logic, an "it," a drive, that is utterly independent of waking-being, with its causal linkages, and indeed not even observed by it. The abundant proliferation of primitive peoples is a *natural phenomenon,* which is not even thought about, still less judged as to its utility or the reverse. When reasons have to be put forward at all in a question of life, life itself has become questionable. At that point begins prudent limitation of the number of births. In the Classical world the practice was deplored by Polybius as the ruin of Greece, and yet even at his date it had long been established in the great cities; in subsequent Roman times it became appallingly general. At first explained by the economic misery of the times, very soon it ceased to explain itself at all. And at that point, too, in Buddhist India as in Babylon, in Rome as in our own cities, a man's choice of the woman who is to be, not mother of his children as amongst peasants and primitives, but his own "companion for life," becomes a problem of mentalities. The Ibsen marriage appears, the "higher spiritual affinity" in which both parties are "free"—free, that is, as intelligences, free from the plantlike urge of the blood to continue itself, and it becomes possible for a Shaw to say "that unless Woman repudiates her womanliness, her duty to her husband, to her children, to society, to the law, and to everyone but herself, she cannot emancipate herself." The primary woman, the peasant woman, is *mother.* The whole vocation towards which she has yearned from childhood is included in that one word. But now emerges the Ibsen woman, the comrade, the heroine of a whole megalopolitan literature from Northern drama to Parisian novel. Instead of children, she has soul-conflicts; marriage is a craft-art for the achievement of "mutual understanding." It is all the same whether the case against children is the American lady's who would not miss a season for anything, or the Parisienne's who fears that her lover would leave her, or an Ibsen heroine's who "belongs to herself"—they all belong to themselves and they are all unfruitful. The same fact, in conjunction with the same arguments, is to be found in the Alexandrian, in the Roman, and, as a matter of course, in every other civilized society—and conspicuously in that in which Buddha grew up. And in Hellenism and in the nineteenth century, as in the times of Lao-Tzu and the Charvaka doctrine, there is an ethic for childless intelligences, and a literature about the inner conflicts of Nora and Nana. The "quiverful," which was still an honourable enough spectacle in the days of Werther, becomes something rather provincial. The father of many children is for the great city a subject for caricature; Ibsen did not fail to note it, and presented it in his *Love's Comedy*.

At this level all Civilizations enter upon a stage, which lasts for centuries, of appalling depopulation. The whole pyramid of cultural man vanishes. It crumbles from the summit, first the world-cities, then the provincial forms, and finally the land itself, whose best blood has incontinently poured into the towns, merely to bolster them up awhile. At the last, only the primitive blood remains, alive, but robbed of its strongest and most promising elements. This residue is the *Fellah type*.

FILMER S. C. NORTHROP (b. 1893), professor emeritus of philosophy and law at Yale University, examined the cultural differences between East and West in various books and articles. Here, he reads the mind and reveals the heart of a nation by studying the physiognomy of her capital city's central square. As a philosopher, Northrop sees the soul of a society as being formed by thought and in turn influencing thought, both soul and thought express themselves in art and architecture.*

Filmer S. C. Northrop

The Mind of Mexico

The Sunshine Limited had swerved and twisted through two interrupted nights and a novel but wearisome day from San Antonio to Mexico City. A spirited taxicab had sped by shops and parks reminiscent of Paris, skyscrapers with signs bearing the impress of New York, and past the heavy white marble Palace of the Fine Arts, to stop at the Spanish Hotel Majestic facing the colonial Catholic Cathedral and National Palace, which flank the distinctly Mexican Zócalo, whose lawns and gardens cover the Aztec ruins across the way.

There they were. All within one square mile. Five distinct and unique cultures: ancient Aztec, Spanish colonial, French nineteenth century, Anglo-American economic, and contemporary Mexican. Harmoniously yet competitively diverse and at times so tremendous and incredible that again and again one could hardly believe one's eyes.

Within the last of these cultures, painting as expansive and profound as it is vital and arresting. Frescoes with a form and sweep which would take one to Rome to find their equal. The human figure formed at times, as Justino Fernández has shown, with a skill comparable to that of Michelangelo, Tintoretto, and El Greco. Also, there is the music of Carlos Chavez, not to mention the names of notable poets, sculptors, and architects. Such is the rich culture of Mexico. Possessions of the imagination and the sentiments which, when we pursue them, intimate the meaning not merely of Mexico and Latin

America but also of all America and Europe, providing even a tie and a bridge to Asia.

Two squares from the Cathedral is a former Encarnacion Convent, covering an entire, exceptionally lengthy city block, now a redecorated government building housing the Secretariat of Public Education. This secular public usage of a former seclusive religious compound typifies the influence of the modern democratic and later positivistic French philosophy of Mexico of the nineteenth century upon the Medieval Catholic culture of its colonial period. Passing through its main entrance one finds oneself facing a large, open, primary square patio divided by three levels of open colonnades from a second large, open court beyond. One's attention is caught immediately by the vast expanse of frescoes covering the inner walls of the three levels running entirely around the rectangle formed by the two courts. These frescoes are by Diego Rivera and other contemporary Mexican painters. They depict the history of Mexico, glorifying the native Indian stock and holding up as a human value the application of science to the natural resources of the country freed for the people from both priests and capitalists. Clearly this is the focus into which the culture of the past converges and from which radiates that of the present and the future.

But even this does not exhaust its significance, as the architectural design of the primary patio indicates. The four sides of this square patio with its three levels of colonnades do not meet in visibly right-angled corners. Instead, in each corner a *pan coupé*, or single narrow, vertical, rectangular plane surface running continuously from the stone pavement below to the roof above and facing the center of the court, has been added.

These four verticle-plane truncated-corner surfaces of the patio, masking its right-angled corners and focusing upon its center, give a unity to the square court in all three dimensions. Upon these four upright, smooth stone surfaces are cut four world figures, one only in each truncated corner. Their primary location insures that they signify factors which are very important. These four figures are of Quetzalcoatl, Las Casas, Plato, and the Buddha.

In a country such as Mexico in which aesthetic values are primary, and rarely if ever merely decorative, one soon learns to listen carefully when, with architecture, it is said, "These four men are of primary importance." One realizes of a sudden that one is face to face not merely with the roots of Mexican culture but also with its relations to world culture. . . .

But why these four men? To answer this question is to possess the key to the Mexican and even the Spanish soul.

The presence of Quetzalcoatl and Las Casas is easy to understand. Quetzalcoatl, meaning "plumed serpent," was the major deity of the pre-colonial Aztec inhabitants of the valley of Mexico and the founder of their agriculture and industry. He represents the purely Indian portion of the Mexican soul and culture. Fr. Bartolomé de Las Casas is generally regarded throughout the Latin-American world as the creator of the Spanish colonial culture of the New Spain. Some twenty years before Cortés he was in an expedition under Columbus to the West Indies. In 1502 he was in Haiti and in 1511 in Cuba. Later he resided in Nicaragua, Peru, Guatemala, and Mexico, where he was Bishop of Chiapa. It was he who taught the Indians how to make of the Spanish language, art, and religion, the spontaneous and original creation of their own spirits which we find it to be even today. Las Casas represents the Spanish colonial component of the Mexican spirit.

But why Plato and the Buddha? Were this a building of similar importance north of the Rio Grande or in Europe the Buddha rather than the Christ, would be missing. Even the presence of Plato presents a problem. To be sure, Mexico is a predominantly Catholic country, and Catholic theology is rooted in the science and philosophy of the Greeks. But ever since St. Thomas Aquinas was canonized in 1323 it has been Aristotle's philosophy rather than Plato's which has defined orthodox Catholic doctrine. Plato and Buddha present a puzzle, perhaps two puzzles, calling for an explanation. These questions must be kept in mind as one examines the major components of Mexico's culture. . . .

In Plato's philosophy there are two "ground principles," as his famous lecture *On the Good* specifically stated: one, the rational, mathematical, formal principle; the other, the intuitive, immediately apprehended, emotional, aesthetic principle termed "the indeterminate dyad," or the potentially differentiable aesthetic continuum. The nature of the rational principle is investigated in the *Republic,* the nature of the emotional aesthetic principle, in the *Phaedrus* and the *Symposium.* In the latter books it is called *éros,* which Jowett renders into English as "frenzy" or "love" or "passion." We are now able to understand why, in the square patio of the Secretariat of Public Education in Mexico City, Plato rather than the more recently orthodox Aristotle stands in its Greek corner. Thanks to Edmundo O'Gorman, we know also that Plato would not be there were not Las Casas there also.

But Plato's teaching contains additional, relevant points. In his dialogue the *Timaeus,* which brings together the aesthetic, emotional *éros* principle of the *Phaedrus* and *Symposium* and the rational, scientific *lógos* principle of the *Republic,* he tells us that the former is the female and the latter the male principle in the nature of things. This is the reason why the emotional, passionate person in the Christian Church's symbolism is the female Virgin and why the doctrinal, rational person in its symbolism is the male Christ, representing the unseen, because only rationally known, God the Father.

Failing to make an important distinction, Plato went on quite arbitrarily to brand the aesthetic, emotional female principle as evil and the male rational principle as good. Consequently, it is to this rational factor, termed God the Father, that the Divine is restricted in the orthodox Christian religion of the West, whether Catholic or Protestant.

This is why one destroys orthodox Christianity when one attacks reason, why the Protestant Church does not allow the Virgin in its symbolism at all, why it tends to be afraid of vivid colors, the passions and the emotions, and why the Catholic Church, when orthodox, whether its orthodoxy be that of the earlier St. Augustine and Plato or the later and current St. Thomas and Aristotle, always insists that the Virgin is not divine immediately in her own right, but only mediately because she is the purely earthly mother of the Christ. This is the reason also, as Henry Adams has suggested in his profound *St. Michel and Chartres,* why, during that period when Abélard's attack had wiped out the Augustinian and Platonic theory of ideas, thereby robbing Christ of his traditional divinity, and before St. Thomas had appeared to restore Christ's divinity by defining it in terms of the rational principle in Aristotle's metaphysics, the

Church at Chartres had no alternative but to fall back upon the Virgin, divine in Her own right, for whom Christ is important solely because he is Her son. During this important interval the Christian religion, acting more wisely than it knew, became identical, as the later chapters of this volume will show, with the religion of the Orient.

A glimmering of the source of the unorthodoxy of Mexico's catholicism is now beginning to dawn upon us. A few more moments with other relevant events, and it will be clear. Salvador de Madariaga did not say, "The essence of the Spanish soul is passion and reason." He omitted the "reason" entirely; it is nothing but passion. Thus the Spanish soul is not orthodox in the Western religious sense of the word. This answers the major question which anyone who reflects upon the history of Spain in Europe should ask himself: Why is it that in its entire history, until very recently, the Spanish soul has never produced one typical Western scientific or philosophical thinker with a logically formulated doctrine such as Euclid's *Elements,* St. Thomas's *Summa,* Newton's *Principia,* Kant's *Critique of Pure Reason,* or Albert Einstein's *General Theory of Relativity?* The answer is given in Salvador de Madariaga's definition of the Spanish spirit: It has followed the passion principle and neglected the rational principle except in its aesthetic, analogical manifestations.

Consider one other fact. It will be recalled that the Medical School of the National University of Mexico is now housed in what was formerly the Inquisition Building of the Dominican Order. This association between the Inquisition and the Dominicans is not accidental. The Inquisition attacked the unorthodox. The Dominican Order is the Order to which St. Thomas, the definer of orthodoxy, belonged. Studies by Mexican scholars show that the Catholic colleges which openly taught the modern unorthodox doctrines were those of the Order of the Jesuits. This is the one Order in the Catholic Church of purely Spanish origin. Being Spanish, religion for the Spanish Mexican Jesuits was, to use the words of Salvador de Madariaga, "an individual passion like love, jealousy, or ambition." Hence the doctrine, whether orthodox or unorthodox, was irrelevant. Consequently, providing the Church flourished at the time, it was unimportant to the Jesuits whether the doctrine which was taught was that of St. Thomas, Descartes, or Voltaire. This neglect of doctrine accounts also for the frenzied, pragmatic expendiency usually associated with the Jesuits.

The unorthodoxy at Guadalupe and in the greater devotion to the Virgin than to the Christ in the other Mexican churches also gains its explanation: It is in the Indian and the Spanish feeling that the aesthetic intuition and passion are the primary and important factors in human nature and in religion, toghether with the Spanish Jesuits' resort to pragmatic expediency due to the neglect of the rational principle.

Christians, both Protestant and Catholic, and pragmatists, as well as all others who for one reason or another have neglected theory, will do well to reflect upon this bit of history. Apparently the Catholics have done so, for in the United States and in Mexico today one finds them strictly orthodox in their teaching. Even the Jesuits, having seen their own monasteries and colleges taken away as a consequence of their teaching of Descartes and Voltaire, seem to have learned their lesson. This shows in the present revival of neo-Scholasticism. Throughout the whole of Latin America there is an interest in the writings of its leading contemporary exponent, Jacques Maritain.

It may be safely predicted, however, that this reaction, commendable as it is because of its appreciation of clearly defined and consistently developed religious doctrine, will not go very far. In fact, since this paragraph was first written, popular protest has forced the removal of the Thomist Rector of the University of Mexico. The basis of contemporary religious preaching and practice upon principle rather than upon temporary expediency or the passing and conflicting whims of the moment must be accomplished by determining the basic theoretical assumptions of *contemporary* knowledge and then pursuing them to their theological and cultural consequences, not by attempting to return to the inadequate Aristotelian science and its attendantly inadequate Thomistic theology of the Middle Ages. Authoritative and excellent as it was for the fourteenth century, it will not do for our time, which must include not merely diverse modern as well as medieval Western values but also Oriental insights as well.

But even Mexican Catholicism itself will not sustain neo-Thomism. The vital part of the Mexican religion is that exhibited at Guadalupe and in the artistry dedicated to the Virgin in the Spanish colonial churches. Both of these manifestations, as the previous consideration of them has shown, are unorthodox. They give expression to a religion of passion based on the female *éros* principle in the nature of things, not to the purely male rational principle of the Aristotelian science and the divine revelation of St. Thomas. Moreover, they both insist that the aesthetically immediate, emotionally moving Virgin is not a mere symbol, pointing beyond herself through the Christ-child to God the Father, but is Divine in Her own right. Thereby, they depart not merely from the present orthodoxy of St. Thomas and Aristotle but also from the earlier Catholic orthodoxy of St. Augustine and Plato and from Christianity generally.

Nowhere does this exclusiveness and intrinsic goodness of the female aesthetic component in the nature of things show itself more markedly than in José Orozco's fresco "Omniscience." Since the time of Plato, omniscience, of all things, has been identified with the male theoretical component in human knowledge. Consequently only God the Father, not the Virgin Mary, was omniscient. Nevertheless, in th^ Orozco fresco in the House of Tiles, omniscience is symbolized by the figure of the human female . . .

Again, it is not the mathematically and logically formulated theoretical knowledge itself, but only the passionately felt, aesthetic materials in which the scientific theory is conveyed, that interests the Spanish-Indian portion of the Mexican spirit. To produce a theoretically oriented thinker one must first erect a hypothesis taking one beyond the immediately experienced, passionately felt aesthetic component of the nature of things and then concentrate one's attention upon the abstract, logical, and mathematical consequences of its assumptions, returning to the world of aesthetically immediate, passionate experience only later, if at all. That this is uncongenial to the Spaniard, José Orozco has suggested in his painting "The Scientist," in the New School for Social Research in New York City. Conversely, because the Spaniard's attention is absorbed with the passionately felt aesthetic materials which are as much imaginative as sensuous, his genius shows itself in mystics like St. Theresa and the poetic St. John of the

Cross, painters like El Greco and Picasso, individual discoverers like Balboa and Cortés, and heroes of the imagination like Sancho Panza and Don Quixote.

One final question remains: Why does the Spanish soul behave in this manner? In doing so, it has adopted as good in itself the emotional, aesthetic female component of things which Plato and the Christian Church following him designated as mere symbol and as evil. This question can be properly answered only when we have examined more in detail the roots of Western civilization and of Eastern culture. Certain points to be demonstrated later may, however, be noted now. Plato, in his famous lecture on the Good, even when designating the female aesthetic component as evil, nevertheless indicated it to be an ultimate, irreducible factor, one of the two "ground principles [ἀρχαί] of all things." As the sequel will show, it is with this female, compassionate, aesthetic component that the good and the divine in the philosophy and religion of the Orient are identified. In fact, it is likely that this female ground principle in Plato's philosophy was not original with Plato but came to him from the East.

It is significant that the medieval culture of Spain was created as much by an Arabian invasion from the East as by indigenous influences within the West. Also, men everywhere, as the Orientals and the ancient Aztecs indicate, begin with the aesthetic emotional principle in the nature of things and come to the rational principle, which is the great discovery of Western science and philosophy and its religion of God the Father, only later, if at all. One feels the beauty of the sunset before one learns of the internal constitution of the stars. The most typical representative in the Orient of this purely intuitive, compassionate, aesthetic view of life is the Buddha.

Thus it is that Quetzalcoatl, Las Casas, and Plato guide us to the reason for the presence beside them of the Buddha rather than the Christ in the fourth truncated corner of the square patio of the Secretariat of Public Education in Mexico City.

Philosophers of history and historians of the world have always tried to find the spirit of an age or civilization in the art, architecture, literature, music, philosophy, religion, political and social institutions, as well as the economy they produced or consumed. Their systems have usually been charged with failure to digest the mass of material and take all data into account. ARNOLD J. TOYNBEE contends that, as the pyramid of a civilization is being built up, it reduces itself to a representative sample and reveals a simple outline on the basis of which the elaborate structures of human society rise and collapse.*

Arnold J. Toynbee

History, Science, and Fiction

There are three different methods of viewing and presenting the objects of our thought, and, among them, the phenomena of human life. The first is the ascertainment and recording of "facts"; the second is the elucidation, through a comparative study of the facts ascertained, of general "laws"; the third is the artistic re-creation of the facts in the form of "fiction." It is generally assumed that the ascertainment and recording of facts is the technique of history, and that the phenomena in the province of this technique are the social phenomena of civilizations; that the elucidation and formulation of general laws is the technique of science, and that, in the study of human life, the science is anthropology and the phenomena in the province of the scientific technique are the social phenomena of primitive societies; and, lastly, that fiction is the technique of the drama and the novel, and that the phenomena in the province of this technique are the personal relations of human beings. All this, in essentials, is to be found in the works of Aristotle.

The distribution of the three techniques between the three departments of study is, however, less watertight than might be supposed. History, for example, does not concern itself with the recording of all the facts of human life. It leaves alone the facts of social life in primitive societies, from which anthropology elucidates its "laws"; and it hands over to biography the facts of individual lives—though nearly all individual lives that are of

*From *A Study of History,* Volumes I–VI, by Arnold J. Toynbee, abridged by D. C. Somervell. Copyright 1946 by Oxford University Press. Reprinted by permission. Pp. 43–47.

sufficient interest and importance to make them seem worth recording have been lived, not in primitive societies, but in one or other of those societies in process of civilization which are conventionally regarded as history's province. Thus history concerns itself with some but not all the facts of human life; and, on the other hand, besides recording facts, history also has recourse to fictions and makes use of laws.

History, like the drama and the novel, grew out of mythology, a primitive form of apprehension and expression in which—as in fairy tales listened to by children or in dreams dreamt by sophisticated adults—the line between fact and fiction is left undrawn. It has, for example, been said of the *Iliad* that anyone who starts reading it as history will find that it is full of fiction but, equally, anyone who starts reading it as fiction will find that it is full of history. All histories resemble the *Iliad* to this extent, that they cannot entirely dispense with the fictional element. The mere selection, arrangement and presentation of facts is a technique belonging to the field of fiction, and popular opinion is right in its insistence that no historian can be "great" if he is not also a great artist; that the Gibbons and Macaulays are greater historians than the "Dryasdusts" (a name coined by Sir Walter Scott— himself a greater historian in some of his novels than in any of his "histories") who have avoided their more inspired confrères' factual inaccuracies. In any case, it is hardly possible to write two consecutive lines of historical narrative without introducing such fictitious personifications as "England," "France," "the Conservative Pary," "the Church," "the Press" or "public opinion." Thucydides dramatized "historical" personages by putting "fictitious" speeches and dia-

logues into their mouths, but his *oratio recta,* while more vivid, is really no more fictional than the laboured *oratio obliqua* in which the moderns present their composite photographs of public opinion.

On the other hand history has taken into her service a number of ancillary sciences which formulate general laws not about primitive societies but about civilizations: e.g. economics, political science and sociology.

Though it is not necessary to our argument, we might demonstrate that, just as history is not innocent of using the techniques associated with science and fiction, so science and fiction by no means confine themselves to what are supposed to be their own techniques. All sciences pass through a stage in which the ascertainment and recording of facts is the only activity open to them, and the science of anthropology is only just emerging from that phase. Lastly, the drama and the novel do not present fictions, complete fictions and nothing but fictions regarding personal relationships. If they did, the product, instead of deserving Aristotle's commendation that it was "truer and more philosophical than history," would consist of nonsensical and intolerable fantasies. When we call a piece of literature a work of fiction we mean no more than that the characters could not be identified with any persons who have lived in the flesh, nor the incidents with any particular events that have actually taken place. In fact, we mean that the work has a fictitious personal foreground; and, if we do not mention that the background is composed of authentic social facts, that is simply because this seems so self-evident that we take it for granted. Indeed, we recognize that the highest praise we can give to a good work of fiction is to say that it is "true of life," and that "the author shows a profound understanding of human nature." To be more particular: if the novel deals with a fictitious family of Yorkshire woollen-manufacturers, we might praise the author by saying that he evidently knows his West Riding mill-towns through and through.

None the less, the Aristotelian distinction between the techniques of history, science and fiction remains valid in a general way, and we shall perhaps see why this is so if we examine these techniques again, for we shall find that they differ from each other in their suitability for dealing with "data" of different quantities. The ascertainment and record of particular facts is all that is possible in a field of study where the data happen to be few. The elucidation and formulation of laws is both possible and necessary where the data are too numerous to tabulate but not too numerous to survey. The form of artistic creation and expression called fiction is the only technique that can be employed or is worth employing where the data are innumerable. Here, as between the three techniques, we have an intrinsic difference of a quantitative order. The techniques differ in their utility for handling different quantities of data. Can we discern a corresponding difference in the quantities of the data that actually present themselves in the respective fields of our three studies?

To begin with the study of personal relations, which is the province of fiction, we can see at once that there are few individuals whose personal relations are of such interest and importance as to make them fit subjects for that record of particular personal facts which we call biography. With these rare exceptions students of human life in the field of personal relations are confronted with innumerable examples of universally familiar experiences. The very idea of an exhaustive recording of them is an absurdity. Any formulation of their "laws" would be intolerably platitudinous or intolerably crude. In such circumstances the data cannot be significantly expressed except in some notation which gives an intuition of the infinite in finite terms; and such a notation is fiction.

Having now found, in quantitative terms, at least a partial explanation of the fact that, in the study of personal relations, the technique of fiction is normally employed, let us see if we can find similar explanations for the normal employment of the law-making technique in the study of primitive societies and the fact-finding technique in the study of civilizations.

The first point to observe is that both these other studies are concerned with human relations, but not with the relations of the familiar, personal kind which come within the direct experience of every man, woman and child. The social relations of human beings extend beyond the farthest possible range of personal contacts, and these impersonal relations are maintained through social mechanisms called institutions. Without institutions societies could not exist. Indeed, societies themselves are simply institutions of the highest kind. The study of societies and the study of institutional relations are one and the same thing.

We can see at once that the quantity of data confronting students of institutional relations between people is very much smaller than the quantity confronting students of people's personal relations. We can see further that the quantity of recorded institutional relations that are relevant to the study of primitive societies will be much greater than the quantity of those relevant to the study of "civilized" societies, because the number of known primitive societies   runs to over 650, whereas our survey of societies in process of civilization has enabled us to identify no more than, at the outside, twenty-one. Now 650 examples, while far from necessitating the employment of fiction, are just enough to enable the student to make a beginning with the formulation of laws. On the other hand, students of a phenomenon of which only a dozen or two dozen examples are known are discouraged from attempting more than a tabulation of facts; and this, as we have seen, is the stage in which "history" has remained so far.

At first sight it may seem a paradox to assert that the quantity of data which students of civilizations have at their command is inconveniently small, when our modern historians are complaining that they are overwhelmed by the mass of their materials. But it remains true that the facts of the highest order, the "intelligible fields of study," the *comparable units* of history, remain inconveniently few for the application of the scientific technique, the elucidation and formulation of laws. None the less, at our own peril, we intend to hazard the attempt, and the results of it are embodied in the remainder of this book.

BROOKS ADAMS (1848–1927), great-grandson and grandson of two American presidents, son of an outstanding diplomat, and brother of an equally distinguished historian, foretold the end of the British Empire in *America's Economic Supremacy* (1900), the decline of France in *The New Empire* (1902), and in *The Degradation of Democratic Dogma* (1919) the fall of the United States, and with them, Western civilization. In *The Law of Civilization and Decay* (1896) Adams thought he had found the basis of the rise and fall of civilizations in a few scientific and economic laws which governed the loss of energy. Adams was the first American who systematically based his history of Western civilization on economic evidence.*

Brooks Adams

The Law of Civilization and Decay

The value of history lies not in the multitude of facts collected, but in their relation to each other, and in this respect an author can have no larger responsibility than any other scientific observer. If the sequence of events seems to indicate the existence of a law governing social development, such a law may be suggested, but to approve or disapprove of it would be as futile as to discuss the moral bearings of gravitation.

Some years ago, when writing a sketch of the history of the colony of Massachusetts Bay, I became deeply interested in certain religious aspects of the Reformation, which seemed hardly reconcilable with the theories usually advanced to explain them. After the book had been published, I continued reading theology,

and, step by step, was led back, through the schoolmen and the crusades, to the revival of the pilgrimage to Palestine, which followed upon the conversion of the Huns. As ferocious pagans, the Huns had long closed the road to Constantinople; but the change which swept over Europe after the year 1000, when Saint Stephen was crowned, was unmistakable; the West received an impulsion from the East. I thus became convinced that religious enthusiasm, which, by stimulating the pilgrimage, restored communication between the Bosphorus and the Rhine, was the power which produced the accelerated movement culminating in modern centralization.

Meanwhile I thought I had discovered not only that faith, during the eleventh,

*From Brooks Adams, *The Law of Civilization and Decay* (New York: Alfred A. Knopf, 1959), pp. 57–61.

twelfth, and early thirteenth centuries, spoke by preference through architecture, but also that in France and Syria, at least, a precise relation existed between the ecclesiastical and military systems of building, and that the one could not be understood without the other. In the commercial cities of the same epoch, on the contrary, the religious idea assumed no definite form of artistic expression, for the Gothic never flourished in Venice, Genoa, Pisa, or Florence, nor did any pure school of architecture thrive in the mercantile atmosphere. Furthermore, commerce from the outset seemed antagonistic to the imagination, for a universal decay of architecture set in throughout Europe after the great commercial expansion of the thirteenth century; and the inference I drew from these facts was, that the economic instinct must have chosen some other medium by which to express itself. My observations led me to suppose that the coinage might be such a medium, and I ultimately concluded that, if the development of a mercantile community is to be understood, it must be approached through its money.

Another conviction forced upon my mind, by the examination of long periods of history, was the exceedingly small part played by conscious thought in moulding the fate of men. At the moment of action the human being most invariably obeys an instinct, like an animal; only after action has ceased does he reflect.

These controlling instincts are involuntary, and divide men into species distinct enough to cause opposite effects under identical conditions. For instance, impelled by fear, one type will rush upon an enemy, and another will run away; while the love of women or of money has stamped certain races as sharply as ferocity or cunning has stamped the lion or the fox.

Like other personal characteristics, the peculiarities of the mind are apparently strongly hereditary, and, if these instincts be transmitted from generation to generation, it is plain that, as the external world changes, those who receive this heritage must rise or fall in the social scale, according as their nervous system is well or ill adapted to the conditions to which they are born. Nothing is commoner, for example, than to find families who have been famous in one century sinking into obscurity in the next, not because the children have degenerated, but because a certain field of activity which afforded the ancestor full scope, has been closed against his offspring. Particularly has this been true in revolutionary epochs such as the Reformation; and families so situated have very generally become extinct.

When this stage had been reached, the Reformation began to wear a new aspect, but several years elapsed before I saw whither my studies led. Only very slowly did a sequence of cause and effect take shape in my mind, a sequence wholly unexpected in character, whose growth resembled the arrangement of the fragments of an inscription, which cannot be read until the stones have been set in a determined order. Finally, as the historical work neared an end, I perceived that the intellectual phenomena under examination fell into a series which seemed to correspond, somewhat closely, with the laws which are supposed to regulate the movements of the material universe.

Theories can be tested only by applying them to facts, and the facts relating to successive phases of human thought, whether conscious or unconscious, constitute history; therefore, if intellectual phenomena are evolved in a regular sequence, history, like matter, must be governed by law. In support of such a conjecture, I venture to offer an hypothesis by which to classify a few of the more interesting intellectual phases through which human society must, apparently, pass, in its oscillations between barbarism and civilization, or, what amounts to the same thing, in its movement from a condition of physical dispersion to one of concentration. The accompanying volume contains the evidence which suggested the hypothesis, although, it seems hardly necessary to add, an essay of this size on so vast a subject can only be regarded as a suggestion.

The theory proposed is based upon the accepted scientific principle that the law of force and energy is of universal application in nature, and that animal life is one of the outlets through which solar energy is dissipated.

Starting from this fundamental proposition, the first deduction is, that, as human societies are forms of animal life, these societies must differ among themselves in energy, in proportion as nature has endowed them, more or less abundantly, with energetic material.

Thought is one of the manifestations of human energy, and among the earlier and simpler phases of thought, two stand conspicuous—Fear and Greed. Fear, which, by stimulating the imagination, creates a belief in an invisible world, and ultimately develops a priesthood; and Greed, which dissipates energy in war and trade.

Probably the velocity of the social movement of any community is proportionate to its velocity; therefore, as human movement is accelerated, societies centralize. In the earlier stages of concentration, fear appears to be the channel through which energy finds the readiest outlet; accordingly, in primitive and scattered communities, the imagination is vivid, and the mental types produced are religious, military, artistic. As consolidation advances, fear yields to greed, and the economic organism tends to supersede the emotional and martial.

Whenever a race is so richly endowed with the energetic material that it does not expend all its energy in the daily struggle for life, the surplus may be stored in the shape of wealth; and this stock of stored energy may be transferred from community to community, either by conquest, or by superiority in economic competition.

However large may be the store of energy accumulated by conquest, a race must, sooner or later, reach the limit of its martial energy, when it must enter on the phase of economic competition. But, as the economic organism radically differs from the emotional and martial, the effect of economic competition has been, perhaps invariably, to dissipate the energy amassed by war.

When surplus energy has accumulated in such bulk as to preponderate over productive energy, it becomes the controlling social force. Thenceforward, capital is autocratic, and energy vents itself through those organisms best fitted to give expression to the power of capital. In this last stage of consolidation, the economic, and, perhaps, the scientific intellect is propagated, while the imagination fades, and the emotional, the martial, and the artistic types of manhood decay. When a social velocity has been attained at which the waste of energetic material is so great that the martial and imaginative stocks fail to reproduce themselves, intensifying competition appears to generate two extreme economic types,—the usurer in his most formidable aspect, and the peasant whose nervous system is best adapted to thrive on scanty nutriment. At length a point must be reached when pressure can go no further, and then, perhaps, one of two results may follow: A stationary period may supervene, which may last until ended by war, by exhaustion, or by both combined, as seems to have been the case with the Eastern Empire; or, as in the Western, disintegration may set in, the civilized population may perish, and a reversion may take place to a primitive form or organism.

The evidence, however, seems to point to the conclusion that, when a highly centralized society disintegrates, under the pressure of economic competition, it is because the energy of the race has been exhausted. Consequently, the survivors of such a community lack the power necessary for renewed concentration, and must probably remain inert until supplied with fresh energetic material by the infusion of barbarian blood.

ALFRED L. KROEBER (1876–1960), born in Hoboken, New Jersey, was professor of anthropology at the University of California, Berkeley, and founded the American Anthropological Association (1917). Kroeber became a legend in 1911 when he befriended Ishi, the survivor of an Indian tribe, who had stepped from the Stone Age into the twentieth century bringing along a first-hand knowledge of man's way of life before the birth of civilization. Besides doing spadework in anthropology, Kroeber investigated the rise and decline of creative genius among the cultures of the world. Although he approached their styles statically and statistically, Kroeber possessed a sympathetic understanding of historical attempts at apprehending civilizations.*

Alfred L. Kroeber

Historical Attempts at Apprehending Civilizations

Monistic Approaches

We come now to consideration of diachronic[1] attempts at apprehending civilizations. These may be divided into monistic and pluralistic approaches. This seems like a simple division of convenience, but it is more. The monistic approach tends also to be unilinear; its organization inclines toward separation of stages; and the idea of progress is usually prominent. Recognition of stages in turn tends toward systematization. Indeed it is evident that this line of

thought is philosophical and that it emanates from philosophers or from those with a philosophic approach. Thinking along this line first took shape with Voltaire, unless one is ready to include Vico as a predecessor. It was Voltaire who coined the term "philosophy of history" and who first put the whole area of thought vividly before large numbers of people.

With his superb gift of narration, it is perhaps not surprising that a larger part of Voltaire's "philosophy of history" is actual history than it is philosophy. He did not use the noun "civilization" (though he did employ the corresponding verb and participle) but it is evident that he was *de facto* dealing largely with civilization as his fundamental concept. The

[1] *Diachronic* designates the comprehension of a culture as it unfolds itself through time. Kroeber himself as well as his fellow anthropologists Ruth Benedict and Margaret Mead employ a *synchronic* method, "treating a whole-culture as of a given moment, statically instead of historically"—Ed.

*From A. L. Kroeber, *An Anthropologist Looks at History* (Berkeley and Los Angeles: University of California Press, 1963), pp. 74–83. Reprinted by permission of The Regents of the University of California.

title of his most systematic work varies, in its parts, its whole and its different editions, between *Philosophy of History* and *Essay on the Customs and Spirit of Nations.* With all his passion for enlightenment, Voltaire did not make a formal division of human history into successive steps or stages. This was first done by his successors. From our point of view Voltaire may perhaps be defined as a superb historian and man of letters who *en passant* reflected on enlightenment and unenlightenment and who engaged in some penetrating and cultivated but unsystematic philosophizing.

With Hegel and Comte we are definitely in the realm of outlines of universal history subsumed in three successive stages of progress. Of Hegel's posthumous work on the subject, first published in 1837, *Philosophy of History*, it is probably characteristic that the word "civilization" occurs in the book only once. Concern is with the much more transcendental entity "spirit'; and its three stages of self-liberation. Hegel was capable of actute insights into the events of history, but he was not interested in developing them concretely except in the line of one idea. His inclination is away from particularizing about specific cultures or nations: he remains floating on a level above them.

Auguste Comte used to be hailed as the father of sociology, although modern sociologists have veered away from such ascription. He did coin the name sociology, and he envisaged a hierarchy of sciences with sociology as the capstone. His three progressive stages of human development are not concerned with liberty, as are Hegel's, but with methods of human thinking: the mythological, metaphysical, and positive-scientific. Beyond this simplistic tripartition, Comte's text is strewn perhaps more richly than Hegel's with specific historic judgments and insights; but these are only loosely woven into his systematic fabric.

Among our contemporaries, Northrop and Sorokin may be mentioned as belonging to the monistic tradition. In both of them, acceptance and ultimate solution of the problems of civilization are achieved by balancing of antithetical factors. Northrop's duality is between an aesthetically immediate component and a theoretical one, in the civilizations respectively of the East and of the West. Disharmonies in civilization result from overbalance of one or the other factor, and harmony is to be effected by their reconciliation and integration.

Sorokin's dualism is not framed spatially but temporally. He sees a major cyclic swing of the pendulum between long-term ideational and sensate "supersystems," relieved only by occasional brief transitions of idealism or of breakdown. Sorokin's two phases are essentially descriptive, and he documents them with masses of chronologically dated cultural products. On the basis of his own voluminous substantiating evidence, his "ideational superphase," as it might well be called instead of his own "ideational supersystem," corresponds to the usually accepted formative or developmental stage of major civilizations, and his "sensate" to the fully matured and dissolving stage.

Sorokin is meticulous in distinguishing culture or civilization from society within the sociocultural realm, whenever the distinction is called for. On the other hand, he wholly denies integrational identity to cultures and civilizations, and looks upon them as mere spatial collocations or "congeries." He does grant integration, and therewith a degree of autonomy or identity, to what he calls "cultural systems," namely certain segments of cultures such as art, science, religion, and ethics. He also sees integration pervading his idea-tional and sensate supersystems which transcend cultures. This unusual position of Sorokin of denying integration to the usually accepted major entities of history, its "nations" or civilizations, while allow-ing integration to exist both in topical segments of civilizations and in certain qualitative and recurrent attitudes or out-looks that endure through and beyond civilizations—this anomalous position I can only see as somehow connected with Sorokin's propensity to erect a formal philosophic system. For instance, his 1947 book *Society, Culture, and Person-ality: Their Structure and Dynamics* is subtitled *A System of General Sociology.*

Northrop is a philosopher by profession who is strongly interested in cultures and their values.

Pluralistic Approaches

In a diachronic, pluralistic approach to the interpretation of civilizations, the philosophic cast or slant recedes, as is to be expected, before the empirical. The plu-ralistic construals are comparative; and may be described as attempts to work out a natural history of civilizations.

The line opens with Herder, a Baltic German born fifty years later than Vol-taire, influenced by him, but of a funda-mentally different temperament. Outside German literature as well as within it, Herder's influence has been most impor-tant as a critic and as a stimulator of folk-loristic and non-classical interests. His propensity was for the remote and exotic and anonymous: he was an eighteenth-century romantic. His main work is called *Ideas on the Philosophy of the History of Mankind.* The derivation from Voltaire is obvious in the title; but the scope of the work is surprising. Only the second half of the book settles down to an actual trac-ing of the history of the known peoples of

the world, with primary emphasis on their cultures. The story begins with East Asia, goes on to western Asia, to Greece, to Rome, to the marginal peoples of Europe, and so on, the last of its ten sections being concerned with Europe since the Cru-sades. The first half of the book is devoted to providing a genuine natural history, a history of our planet as the setting of hu-man history. The first section is astronom-ical and geological. The next two are botanical and zoological. Then the struc-tures, functions, organs, and energies of man are considered, followed by the varieties of his racial physiques and the environmental influences bearing on him. Then follows what might be fairly trans-lated in modern terminology as a theory of human culture, which Herder variably calls "humanity" *(Humanität),* "tradi-tion," or "culture" *(Cultur).* This pre-liminary half of the book ends with a discussion of the origins of man in Asia. This sets man in his place in the world. Only then does the "philosophy" of his history of culture begin to be recounted.

This summary suffices to suggest a cer-tain diffuseness, a quality with which Herder has often been charged. But it also indicates his interest in bases as well as in culminations, in nature as something larger that includes man, in multiple human efforts which, however, can also be viewed together as a totality of culture; and a recognition of all creative cultural products as possessing significance, equally so whether they have or have not led to our own modern civilization.

The Russian Nicolai Danilevsky made a more systematic attempt to treat the greater civilizations in the manner of nat-ural history, being trained as a biologist, in botany and ichthyology. He was also a pan-Slavist, and motivated national-istically to try to apply biological method to human history. His endeavor appeared in the book called *Russia and Europe*, first published in 1869 in a journal and two years later in book form. Danilevsky was evidently impressed by the transience of civilization, an old idea which underlies Gibbon's *Decline and Fall*, as well as numerous eighteenth- and nineteenth-century reflections on the succession and lack of duration of "nations" or "empires." As a pan-Slavist, Danilevsky was inspired by the evidences which he discerned of the decline and impending death of West European civilization, to which he saw as successor a Slavic civilization led by Russia. This is surely not a promising soil in which to expect the development of sound ideology accounting generically for civilizations in history; but Danilevsky's theory can readily be disentangled from his propagandist interests. He recognizes, besides an ethnographic pool of the pre-literate peoples, ten major civilizations in the Old World, plus two that perished in Mexico and Peru, with the Slavs as about to constitute the thirteenth. Each of these civilizations he attempts to construe as a "culture-historical type," a concept evidently based on the biological types of Cuvier. But, whereas the Cuvierian types are plans of fundamental biological organization, and are the pre-evolutionistic equivalent of phyla or grand lines of genetic descent containing innumerable variations, the culture-historical types of Danilevsky each consist of a single example only. Nevertheless Danilevsky's approach is commonsense and empirical. The result is that he sees his civilizations as separate entities, although running roughly parallel courses. In these two points he anticipated Spengler, and it is not wholly clear whether Spengler was influenced by Danilevsky directly or indirectly or not at all. Danilevsky is also somewhat simplistic in characterizing the growth and decay

of civilizations as parallel to the growth and decay of individual plants or organisms. He evidently sees this resemblance as something to be taken for granted on the basis of the outward analogy. But at any rate he does not press beyond the analogy, nor endeavor to assign organic causes to the cultural growth and dissolution process.

With Spengler we encounter a very strong sense of style. He perceives the distinctive qualities of major civilizations with unusual sensitivity—sometimes even forcing imaginary distinctions. This is the easier for him because he recognizes only some six or eight civilizations. The pre-literate ones do not exist as cultures; the intermediate ones he disregards. He also cuts out from consideration what would ordinarily be construed as the later half or more of cultures, their period of maturity and decline. All this portion of their course he looks upon as merely fossilized noncreative culture, which he labels civilization, and refuses to deal with as being in "culture." Spengler's whole intellectual approach would have broken down if he had attempted to apply it to 21 or 29 separate cultures such as those of Toynbee. Throughout, he is given to simplifying situations and especially to exaggerating them.

In the same way he insists that his few genuine cultures are completely and totally integrated, without residuum. They each show a particular pervasive style in all their activities and products. If Spengler had limited himself to seeing some trend toward an integrated and coherent style in each civilization, many of us would be much readier to agree with him.

A corollary of the complete integration which he postulates is that separate cultures are impermeable toward one another. He makes an argument that they do not transfer content one from the other, or if they do, it is utterly changed, so that it can no longer be spoken of as the same content. This of course is simply contrary to the facts of all culture history, which, if it shows anything demonstrates the tremendous amount of cultural content that has been not only transmitted by tradition internally within cultures but has spread cross-culturally.

A result of this gross exaggeration by Spengler is that his cultures become monads; they cannot take anything one from the other; they cannot influence one another; each runs its own course which is completely self-sufficient and unitary. They are something like Democritan atoms except that they perish of themselves, while new ones arise out of nothing.

It is in stylistic keeping with the picture that Spengler paints, that as his cultures are eternally separate and non-related, in other words wholly different but equivalent, so he also makes their courses uniform, both as regards birth and rise and fossilization as well as in actual duration. This duration he sets at 1,000 or 1,500 years, according as the prodromal nascent stage of each culture is excluded or included from the reckoning.

That the cultures must live a similar life and must die is a counterpart of Spengler's powerful sense of doom. It is an exaggeration as regards the facts of history, but it heightens the picture. In trying to set up a concept of fate as a substitute for the concept of cause, Spengler again exaggerates. It is true, in dealing only with the history of nations that close agreement as to the causes of particular events is rare as between different historians. Causality in human history is so diverse in kind, and the causes are so many, that it is exceedingly difficult to agree upon their respective roles, or even to ascertain them all. In

actual practice historians aim to select and portray what is "significant" rather than to give definite explanations of why things happened the precise way that they have happened. Of course this is increasingly true as larger and larger units of history are taken as the subject of inquiry, until we come to those greatest units which we call civilizations. Sorokin has pointed out how logico-meaningfulness is a quality better attained by historical research than are causal-functional relations. One may quarrel with his somewhat awkward terms, but there is little question that, especially in the realm of culture, the significance of historical phenomena can in general be ascertained more successfully than can their causes or functions.

The whole matter of doom, of course, is an unfortunate distraction because of its heavy emotional weighting. Danilevsky already predicted it, but as a Russian he was an optimist as to the future because Slavdom had not yet matured. Spengler came a half century later and as a German was a European, although a marginal one; and he used breakdown as an aesthetic devise to heighten the picture he painted.

One final criticism that must be made of Spengler is that his study is not really comparative—at least it is not freely comparative. Essentially he has worked out with some elaboration a contrast between the Mediterranean classic civilization and the subsequent Occidental or European one. This viewpoint he admittedly took over largely from Nietzsche. Nietzsche however derives from Goethe, and most of his Apollinian—Dionysian contrast, which Spengler called Apollinian-Faustian, can be found set forth poetically and in full in the second act of the second part of Goethe's *Faust*—the Helena episode.

To this pair of cultures, which he knew well, Spengler added as a tertium quid of a fulcrum an imaginary civilization, the

Magian one, overlapping the two preceding in time as well as in space, although apart from "basic symbols" he has relatively little to say about this third culture. As for China, India, Mesopotamia, and Egypt, Spengler is, when analyzed with care, incredibly meager in substantive content, in what he has actually to report about them. There are some brilliant flashes, but vast silences and darknesses between.

Toynbee is not only a trained historian but the only historian in the group of the pluralistic interpreters of civilizations under consideration. He has reacted with moderation and vast empirical knowledge to the dogmatism and exaggeration of Spengler. But he is also partly derived from Spengler, as shown by his near acceptance of Spengler's Magian culture, which he renames Syriac. He goes far beyond Spengler in refusing to simplify his task by dispensing with inconvenient cultures. His array of them is between 20 and 30, according as some of the more "arrested" or "abortive" ones are or are not included. He arranges all these according as they are derived or partly derived from one another, "affiliated" and "apparented"; and he does not hesitate to view two pulses of civilization in the same area as two separate civilizations—if they are not overwhelmingly repetitive.

Toynbee calls his units sometimes civilizations and sometimes societies. He is really thinking more often in terms of societies, that is, aggregations of men and their minorities and majorities, than he is thinking of cultures. Consequently questions of style hardly obtrude in his work.

He does not deny style, but he does not seriously consider it as such. Also, dealing primarily with men or societies of men, or elite and proletarian groups within the societies, he is necessarily more concerned with events than with configurations of either culture or style. And this in turn brings it about that he deals far more with directly efficient causes that reside in men than with the meaningful patterns that culture assumes. The ultimately significant causality which he finds is that of the moral attitudes of men toward their societies, especially in the privileged minorities.

These are factors pretty far removed from considerations of how far a stylistic unity pervades a culture. The challenge, which when successfully met by society's elite, results in the genesis of a civilization, may be physical or social; if the latter, it is usually the disintegration of a previous society. After a period of prosperity and growth, Toynbee finds that certain events are likely to occur: a time of troubles, a universal state, a universal peace, and final breakdown. It is apparent that all these larger events or states are essentially political and moral. So again Toynbee does not really come to grips with culture; the question of how far this may represent a unified style scarcely arises in his mind.

On the other hand, Toynbee's repetitive sequences of events, his formula of expectable events *a, b, c, d,* disconcerts historians. It is perhaps this which has led to their general resistance to Toynbee's scheme: the opposition is on sound procedural grounds.

JUAN DONOSO-CORTÉS (1809–1853), a descendent of the conqueror of Mexico, was born while his family fled from the Napoleonic invasion of Spain. A child prodigy, he studied philosophy, law, and history and was professor at the University of Salamanca by the age of twenty. Subsequently Donoso-Cortés served as membêr of the diet in Madrid, secretary of state, as well as secretary and tutor to two Spanish queens. After 1848 when he became convinced of the final dissolution of modern civilization, he briefly held ambassadorial posts in Berlin and Paris. Donoso-Cortés contributed to many newspapers and wrote several books on law, history, and diplomacy. His most important was the *Essay on Catholicism, Liberalism and Socialism* (1851), which Metternich considered the last word on the nature of revolution. The excerpts below are from his speech on dictatorship (1849).*

Juan Donoso-Cortés

Speech on Dictatorship

Let us now touch on the causes of this Revolution. The progressive party always finds the same causes for everything. Señor Cortina[1] told us yesterday that revolutions occur because of certain illegalities and because the instincts of the people make them rise in a uniform and spontaneous way against tyrants. Señor Ordax Avecilla told us previously: If you want to avoid revolution, give the hungry bread. Here, in all its subtlety, is the progressive theory: the causes of revolution lie, on the one hand in poverty, and on the other in tyranny. This theory, Gentlemen, is contrary, absolutely contrary, to historical fact. I challenge

anybody to quote me one example of a revolution which has been started and brought to a conclusion by men who were either slaves or hungry. Revolutions are a disease of rich peoples, of free peoples. Slaves formed the greater part of the human race in antiquity: tell me one revolution these slaves ever made.

All that they could do was to forment a few slave wars: but deep-seated revolutions were always the work of wealthy aristocracies. No, Gentlemen, the germ of revolution is not to be found in slavery or poverty; the germ of revolution lies in the desires of the mob, which are overexcited by leaders who exploit them for their own advantage. *You will be like the rich*—such is the formula of Socialist revolutions against the middle classes.

[1] Manuel Cortina y Arenzana (1802–1879), a lawyer from Seville and leader of the Liberal party, was one of the most eloquent speakers of the *Cortes*—Ed.

*From *Catholic Political Thought, 1789–1848,* edited by Béla Menczer. Copyright 1962 by the University of Notre Dame Press. Pp. 166–167, 170–173. This is published in Britain by Burns & Oates Ltd.

You will be like the nobles —such is the formula of the revolutions made by the middle classes against the aristocracy. *You will be like Kings* is the formula of revolutions made by the aristocracy against Kings. Finally, Gentlemen, *You will be like gods* —such was the formula of the first revolt of the first man against God. From Adam, the first rebel, to Proudhon,[2] the last blasphemer, such has been the formula of every revolution. . . .

The cause of all your errors, Gentlemen, lies in your ignorance of the direction which civilisation and the world are taking. You believe that civilisation and the world are advancing, when civilisation and the world are regressing. The world is taking great strides towards the constitution of the most gigantic and destructive despotism which men have ever known. That is the trend of our world and civilisation. I do not need to be a prophet to predict these things; it is enough to consider the fearful picture of human events from the only true viewpoint, from the heights of Catholic philosophy.

There are only two possible forms of control: one internal and the other external; religious control and political control. They are of such a nature that when the religious barometer rises, the barometer of control falls and likewise, when the religious barometer falls, the political barometer, that is political control and tyranny, rises. That is a law of humanity, a law of history. If you want proof, Gentlemen, look at the state of the world, look at the state of society in

---

[2] Pierre Joseph Proudhon (1809–1865) was to the age of Donoso-Cortés what Karl Marx meant for later generations, the embodiment of Socialism. Donoso-Cortés seems to have been aware of the beginnings of Marxism, for in another speech, he said, "Socialism was taught in Germany with the authority of science by people who combined the dignity of high priests with the sharp minds of scribes" — Ed.

the ages before the Cross; tell me what happened when there was no internal or religious control. Society in those days only comprised tyrants and slaves. Give me the name of a single people at this period which possessed no slaves and knew no tyrant. It is an incontrovertible and evident fact, which has never been questioned. Liberty, real liberty, the liberty of all and for all, only came into the world with the Saviour of the world; that again is an incontrovertible fact, recognised even by the Socialists. Yes, the Socialists admit it; they call Jesus divine, they go further, they say they continue the work of Jesus. Gracious Heaven! Continue His work! Those men of blood and vengeance continue the work of Him Who only lived to do good, Who only opened His lips to bless, Who only worked miracles to deliver sinners from their sins and the dead from death; Who in the space of three years accomplished the greatest revolution the world has ever witnessed and that without shedding any blood but His own.

Follow me carefully, I beg you; I am going to present you with the most marvellous parallel which history can offer us. You have seen that in antiquity, when religious control was at its lowest point, for it was non-existent, political control rose to the point of tyranny. Very well then, with Jesus Christ, where religious control is born, political control disappears. This is so true, that when Jesus Christ founded a society with His disciples, that society was the only one which has ever existed without a government. Between Jesus Christ and His disciples there was no other government than the love of the Master for His disciples and the love of the disciples for their Master. You see then, that when the internal control was complete, liberty was absolute.

Let us pursue the parallel. Now come

the apostolic times, which I shall stretch, for the purposes of my plan, from the time of the Apostles, properly speaking, to the period when Christianity mounted the Capitol in the reign of Constantine the Great. At this time, Gentlemen, the Christian religion, that is, the internal religious control, was at its zenith; but in spite of that, as always happens in human societies, a germ began to develop, a mere germ of protection and religious liberty. So, Gentlemen, observe the parallel: with this beginning of a fall in the religious barometer there corresponds the beginning of a rise in the political barometer. There is still no government yet, for government is not yet necessary; but it is already necessary to have the germ of government. In point of fact, in the Christian society of the time, there were no real magistrates, but there were adjudicators and arbitrators who form the germ of government. There was really nothing more than that; the Christians of apostolic times engaged in no lawsuits and never appealed to the Courts: their disputes were settled by the arbitrators. Notice, Gentlemen, how the scope of government is enlarged with the growth of corruption.

Then came feudal times. Religion was still at its zenith during this period, but was vitiated up to a point by human passions. What happened in the political sphere? A real and effective government was already essential; but the weakest kind was good enough. As a result, feudal monarchy was established, the weakest of all kinds of monarchy.

Still pursuing our parallel, we come to the sixteenth century. Then, with the great Lutheran Reformation, with this great scandal which was at the same time political, social and religious, with this act of the intellectual and moral emancipation of the peoples, we see simul-

taneously the growth of the following institutions. In the first place, and immediately, the feudal monarchies became absolute. You believe, Gentlemen, that a monarchy and a government cannot go beyond absolutism. However, the barometer of political control had to rise even higher, because the religious barometer continued to fall: and the political barometer did in fact rise higher. What did they create then? Standing armies. Do you know what standing armies are? To answer that question, it is enough to know what a soldier is: a soldier is a slave in uniform. So you see once again, when religious control falls, political control rises, it rises as high as absolutism and even higher. It was not enough for governments to be absolute; they asked for and obtained the privilege of having a million arms at the service of their absolutism.

That is not all: the political barometer had to continue to rise because the religious barometer kept falling; it rose still higher. What new institution was created then? The governments said: We have a million arms and it is not enough; we need something more, we need a million eyes: and they created the police. That was not the last word in progress: the political barometer and political control had to rise to a higher pitch still, because in spite of everything, the religious barometer kept falling; so they rose higher. It was not enough for the governments to have a million arms and a million eyes; they wanted to have a million ears: and so they created administrative centralisation, by means of which all claims and complaints finally reached the government.

Well, Gentlemen, that was not enough; the religious barometer continued to fall and so the political barometer had to rise higher. And it rose. Governments said:

A million arms, a million eyes and a million ears are not sufficient to control people, we need something more; we must have the privilege of being simultaneously present in every corner of our empire. This privilege also they obtained: the telegraph was invented.

Such, Gentlemen, was the state of Europe and the world when the first rumblings of the most recent revolution intimated to us all that there is still not enough despotism on the earth, since the religious barometer remains below zero. And now the choice between two things lies before us.

I have promised to speak today with complete frankness and I shall keep my word. . . .

In a word, this is the choice we have to make: either a religious reaction will set in, or it will not. If there is a religious reaction, you will soon see that as the religious barometer rises, the political barometer will begin to fall, naturally, spontaneously, without the slightest effort on the part of peoples, governments, or men, until the tranquil day comes when the peoples of the world are free. But if, on the contrary, and this is a serious matter (it is not customary to call the attention of Consultative Assemblies to questions of this nature; but the gravity of events today is my excuse and I think I have your indulgence in this matter); I say again, Gentlemen, that if the religious barometer continues to fall, no man can see whither we are going. I cannot see, Gentlemen, and I cannot contemplate the future without terror. Consider the analogies I have put before you and weigh this question in your minds; if no government was necessary when religious control was at its zenith, and now that

religious control is nonexistent, what form of government is going to be strong enough to quell a revolt? Are not all despotisms equally powerless?

Have I not put my finger into the wound, Gentlemen? Yes, I have, and this is the problem which faces Spain, Europe, humanity and the world.

Notice one thing, Gentlemen. In the ancient world, tyranny was fierce and merciless; yet this tyranny was materially limited, since all States were small and formal relations between States were impossible from every point of view; consequently tyranny on the grand scale was impossible in antiquity, with one exception: Rome. But today, how greatly are things changed! The way is prepared for some gigantic and colossal tyrant, universal and immense; everything points to it. Observe that already moral and material resistance is at an end: all minds are divided, all patriotism is dead. Tell me now whether I am right or wrong to be preoccupied with the coming fate of the world; tell me whether, in dealing with this question, I am not touching upon the real problem.

One thing, and one alone, can avert the catastrophe: we shall not avert it by granting more liberty, more guarantees and new constitutions; we shall avert it if all of us, according to our strength, do our utmost to stimulate a salutary reaction—a religious reaction. Now is this possible, Gentlemen? Yes. But is it likely? I answer in deepest sorrow: I do not think it is likely. I have seen and known many men who returned to their faith after having separated themselves from it; unfortunately, I have never known any nation which returned to the Faith after once it was lost.

FRIEDRICH NIETZSCHE (1844–1900) was the most
stimulating and controversial thinker of the nineteenth
century. He repudiated Greek philosophy, Christianity,
"an uprising of slaves," the Reformation, "the peasant
revolution of the German spirit," and democracy and
socialism, which he considered secularized forms of
Christianity. However, he also repudiated militarism,
and anti-Semitism and suffered vicariously the agonies
of our age. The following fragments are from
Nietzsche's notebooks shortly before his mental
breakdown.*

Friedrich Nietzsche

The Rise of Nihilism
and Return to Nature

What I am now going to relate is the
history of the next two centuries. I shall
describe what will happen, what must
necessarily happen: *the triumph of Nihilism.* This history can be written already;
for necessity itself is at work in bringing
it about. This future is already proclaimed by a hundred different omens;
as a destiny it announces its advent everywhere; for this music of to-morrow all
ears are already pricked. The whole of
our culture in Europe has long been
writhing in an agony of suspense which
increases from decade to decade as if in
expectation of a catastrophe: restless,
violent, helter-skelter, like a torrent that
will *reach its* [end], and refuses to reflect—yea, that even dreads reflection.

On the other hand, the present writer
has done little else, hitherto, than *reflect
and meditate,* like an instinctive philosopher and anchorite, who found his advantage in isolation—in remaining outside, in patience, procrastination, and
lagging behind; like a weighing and
testing spirit who has already lost his way
in every labyrinth of the future; like a
prophetic bird-spirit that *looks backwards*
when it would announce what is to come;
like the first perfect European Nihilist,
who, however, has already outlived
Nihilism in his own soul—who has 'out-
grown, overcome, and dismissed it.

For the reader must not misunderstand
the meaning of the title which has been

*From *The Will to Power* by Friedrich Nietzsche, trans. Anthony M. Ludovici (London: George Allen
& Unwin Ltd, 1909), pp. 1–2, 5–7, 177–178. Reprinted by permission.

given to this Evangel of the Future. *"The Will to Power: An Attempted Transvaluation of all Values"*—with this formula a *counter-movement* finds expression, in regard to both a principle and a mission; a movement which in some remote future will supersede this perfect Nihilism; but which nevertheless regards it as a *necessary step,* both logically and psychologically, towards its own advent, and which positively cannot come, except *on top of* and *out of* it. For, why is the triumph of Nihilism *inevitable* now? Because the very values current amongst us to-day will arrive at their logical conclusion in Nihilism,—because Nihilism is the only possible outcome of our greatest values and ideals,—because we must first experience Nihilism before we can realise what the actual worth of these "values" was. . . . Sooner or later we shall be in need of *new values.*

1. Nihilism is at our door: whence comes this most gruesome of all guests to us?—To begin with, it is a mistake to point to "social evils," "physiological degeneration," or even to corruption as a cause of Nihilism. This is the most straightforward and most sympathetic age that ever was. Evil, whether spiritual, physical, or intellectual, is, in itself, quite unable to introduce Nihilism, *i.e.,* the absolute repudiation of worth, purpose, desirability. These evils allow of yet other and quite different explanations. But there is one *very definite explanation* of the phenomena: Nihilism . . . [nests] in the heart of Christian morals.

2. The downfall of Christianity,—through its morality (which is insuperable), which finally turns against the Christian God Himself (the sense of truth, highly developed through Christianity, ultimately revolts against the falsehood and fictitiousness of all Christian interpretations of the world and its history. The recoil-stroke of "God is Truth" in the fanatical Belief is: "All is false." Buddhism of *action.* . . .).

3. Doubt in morality is the decisive factor. The downfall of the *moral* interpretation of the universe, which loses its *raison d'être* once it has tried to take flight to a Beyond, meets its end in Nihilism. "Nothing has any purpose" (the inconsistency of one explanation of the world, to which men have devoted untold energy,—gives rise to the suspicion that all explanations may perhaps be false). The Buddhistic feature: a yearning for nonentity (Indian Buddhism has no fundamentally moral development at the back of it; that is why Nihilism in its case means only morality not overcome; existence is regarded as a punishment and conceived as an error; error is thus held to be punishment—a moral valuation). Philosophical attempts to overcome the "moral God" (Hegel, *Pantheism*). The vanquishing of popular ideals: the wizard, the saint, the bard. Antagonism of "true" and "beautiful" and "good."

4. Against "purposelessness" on the one hand, against moral valuations on the other: how far has all science and philosophy been cultivated heretofore under the influence of moral judgments? And have we not got the additional factor—the enmity of science, into the bargain? Or the prejudice against science? Criticism of Spinoza. Christian valuations everywhere present as remnants in socialistic and positivistic systems. *A criticism of Christian* morality is altogether lacking.

5. The Nihilistic consequences of present natural science (along with its attempts to escape into a Beyond). Out of its practice there finally *arises* a certain self-annihilation, an antagonistic attitude

towards itself—a sort of anti-scientifical-ity. Since Copernicus man has been roll-ing away from the centre towards x.[1]

6. The Nihilistic consequences of the political and politico-economical way of thinking, where all principles at length become tainted with the atmosphere of the platform: the breath of mediocrity, in-significance, dishonesty, etc. Nationalism. Anarchy, etc. Punishment. Everywhere the *deliverer* is missing, either as a class or as a single man—the justifier.

7. Nihilistic consequences of history and of the "practical historian," *i.e.,* the romanticist. The attitude of art is quite unoriginal in modern life. Its gloominess. Goethe's so-called Olympian State.

8. Art and the preparation of Nihilism. Romanticism (the conclusion of Wagner's *Ring of the Nibelung*).

Christianity is a denaturalisation of gregarious[2] morality: under the power of the most complete misapprehensions and self-deceptions. Democracy is a more natural form of it, and less sown with falsehood. It is a fact that the oppressed, the low, and whole mob of slaves and half-castes, *will prevail.*

First step: they make themselves free—they detach themselves, at first in fancy only; they recognise each other; they make themselves paramount.

Second step: they enter the lists, they demand acknowledgment, equal rights, "Justice."

Third step: they demand privileges (they draw the representatives of power over to their side).

Fourth step: they *alone* want all power, and they *have* it.

There are *three elements* in Christian-ity which must be distinguished: *(a)* the oppressed of all kinds, *(b)* the mediocre of all kinds, *(c)* the dissatisfied and dis-eased of all kinds. The *first* struggle against the politically noble and their ideal; the second contend with the excep-tions and those who are in any way privi-leged (mentally or physically); the third oppose the *natural instinct* of the happy and the sound.

Whenever a triumph is achieved, the second elements steps to the fore; for then Cristianity has won over the sound and happy to its side (as warriors in its cause), likewise the powerful (interested to this extent in the conquest of the crowd) —and now it is the *gregarious instinct,* that *mediocre nature* which is valuable in every respect, that now gets its highest sanction through Christianity. This medi-ocre nature ultimately becomes so con-scious of itself (gains such courage in re-gard to its own opinions), that it arro-gates to itself even *political power. . . .*

Democracy is Christianity *made nat-ural:* a sort of "return to Nature," once Christianity, owing to extreme anti-naturalness, might have been overcome by the opposite valuation. Result: the aristocratic ideal begins to *lose its natural character* ("like the higher man," "noble," "artist," "passion," "knowledge"; Roman-ticism as the cult of the exceptional, genius, etc. etc.).

---

[1] "Since Copernicus man seems to have fallen on to a steep plane—he rolls faster and faster away from the center—whither? into nothingness? into the *thrilling sensation of his own nothingness?*"—Nietzsche wrote in *The Genealogy of Morals* (1887), Third Essay, Section 25—Ed.

[2] "Gregarious" refers to the natural instinct of self-preservation in a herd. In Nietzsche's thought, it is the "gregarious instinct" of the lowest classes, which prevails with the aid and comfort of Chris-tianity—Ed.

VILFREDO PARETO (1848–1923) was born in Paris, the son of an Italian exile who had followed the national revolutionary Mazzini. He returned to Italy with his parents at the age of ten and became director of a railroad company and an engineer in an ironwork; he resided in Florence. In 1893 he was called to the University of Lausanne in French-speaking Switzerland. He was involved in both economics and sociology. In economics, he invented "econometrics." In sociology, he influenced Sorokin. Because of his scholarly opinion that the irrational side of man's actions colored his thoughts, Pareto was both hailed and condemned as forerunner of Fascism. However, he kept aloof from all political movements being amused by their follies.*

Vilfredo Pareto

The Decline of the Old Elite

The elite which is still dominant, consists principally of the bourgeoisie and, to a small extent, of the remnants of the other elites.

When an elite declines, we can generally observe two signs which manifest themselves simultaneously:

1. The declining elite becomes softer, milder, more humane and less apt to defend its own power.

2. On the other hand, it does not lose its rapacity and greed for the goods of others, but rather tends as much as possible to increase its unlawful appropriations and to indulge in major usurpations of the national patrimony.

Thus, on one hand it makes the yoke heavier, and on the other it has less strength to maintain it. These two conditions cause the catastrophe in which the elite perishes, whereas it could prosper if one of them were absent. Thus, if its own strength does not weaken but grows, its appropriations too may increase, and if these decrease, its dominion may, though less frequently, be maintained with a lesser force. Thus the feudal nobility, at the time it arose, could increase its usurpations because its force was growing; thus the Romans and the English elites could, while yielding where yielding was called for, maintain their own power. The French aristocracy on the other hand, eager to maintain its own privileges, and perhaps also to increase them, while its force to defend them was

*Vilfredo Pareto, *The Rise and Fall of the Elites,* Bedminster Press, Totowa, New Jersey, 1968, pp. 67–71. Copyright © 1968, The Bedminster Press. Reprinted by permission. Asterisks within the text indicate that a footnote has been deleted.

diminishing, provoked the violent revolution of the end of the eighteenth century. In short, there must be a certain equilibrium between the power a social class possesses and the force at its disposal to defend it. Domination without that force cannot last.

Elites often become effete. They preserve a certain passive courage, but lack active courage. It is amazing to see how in imperial Rome the members of the elite committed suicide or allowed themselves to be assassinated without the slightest defense, as long as it pleased Caesar. We are equally amazed when we see the nobles of France die on the guillotine, instead of going down fighting, weapon in hand.*

Rome marveled greatly seeing the vigor of the old elite flower anew in Silano. Locked up in Bari, he answered the centurion who tried to persuade him to let his veins be opened *(suadentique venas abrumpere)* that he was ready to die, but also to fight. Although unarmed, he never ceased to defend himself and to strike out as he could with his bare hands, until he fell as it were in combat, pierced by stabs received from the front.*

If Louis XVI had had the spirit of Silano, he would have saved himself and his family, and perhaps spared the nation much blood and pain. Even on August 10 he could still have fought a battle with hope to win. "If the king had wanted to fight he could still have defended himself, he could have saved himself and even won," says Taine.* But the elite of that time resembled the bourgeoisie of today, as can be observed in countries like France, where the democratic evolution is most accentuated. Although Taine speaks of that time, his language precisely describes present conditions in France when he says: "At the end of the 18th century, a horror of blood prevailed in the upper, and even in the middle class; refinement of manners and idyllic dreams had weakened the militant will power (and today again the French bourgeoisie indulges in sweet dreams). Everywhere the magistrates were forgetting that the maintenance of society and civilization is infintely more valuable than the lives of a handful of offenders and fools. They forgot that the primary objective of government, as it is of the police force, is the preservation of order through force."* The same phenomenon could be seen in Rome, where it prepared the downfall of the empire,* and now that it is being repeated for our bourgeoisie, it seems likely that the end will not be different from that which has been observed in the past.*

At present this phenomenon can be seen in almost all the civilized states, but is best observed in France and Belgium, which are more advanced in the radical-socialist evolution and show in some manner the goal toward which the evolution tends in general.

A superficial study is sufficient to show that the dominant class in these countries is weighed down by sentimental and humanitarian tendencies quite similar to those which existed toward the end of the eighteenth century. The sensibility of that class has become almost morbid and threatens to deprive the penal laws of all efficacy. Every day new laws are being devised to help poor thieves and amiable assassins, and where a new law does not exist, a convenient interpretation of the old one will do. At Château-Thierry, a now famous judge simply ignores the law and judicates according to the blind passion of the crowd.*[1] The bourgeoisie resigns itself and remains

---

[1] The "now famous judge" became president of the *Congrès de l'humanité* — Ed.

silent. If another judge wishes to do his duty, he is eyed with distrust and perhaps ridiculed on the stage. In the absence of every repression, the vagabonds have become a real scourge of the countryside; in isolated cottages, they threaten while they beg; or of revenge, or an evil impulse, or simply by imprudence, they burn down the castles of the rich; arson has by now become a frequent occurrence. The authorities look on and remain inactive; they know that if they performed their duty punctiliously the results would be interpellations in Parliament and perhaps the downfall of the Cabinet. Even stranger to watch is the demeanor of the victims, who are silent and resigned, as if faced by an evil to which there is no remedy. The most courageous content themselves with the hope that some general will re-enact the operation of Napoleon III, and, in the process, liberate them from the plague.

The crimes committed during strikes remain unpunished; the judges will sometimes pass a guilty verdict but it is a formal verdict at best, soon to be followed by an acquittal, imposed by the workers or spontaneously conceded by the government "to pacify." The workers have inherited the privilege of the nobleman of the past, they are in fact above the law. They have even a special tribunal of their own, the court of arbitration, which will definitely condemn the "boss" and the "bourgeois" even if these had all the right on their side. Where this parody of justice is being enacted, the honest attorney will advise his client not to seek litigation because he would be sure to lose. Of course, social democracy wishes to extend the jurisdiction of this exceptional tribunal. The ecclesiastic court has been abolished—and the workers' court was born. Athenian democracy, which was ruining the rich through lawsuits, was imitated by the Italian republics, and is now being imitated by modern democracy.* The old elite, when it was in power, did even worse, so that one cannot conclude from these facts anything against one or the other regime;* they are simply signs indicating which class is declining and which is on the rise. Where class *A* enjoys legal privileges and the laws are wrongly interpreted in its favor and against class *B,* it is obvious that *A* has, or is about to have, the advantage over *B,* and vice versa.

The decisions of the jury are also signs in this direction and show that the bourgeoisie adopts the worst sentiments of the common people.

Finally, where a little romance enters the picture, bourgeois sentimentality reveals itself as foolishly wicked. From among many instances, it is sufficient to mention this recent one. A gentleman, who was boyishly sentimental, married a prostitute in order to "rehabilitate" her; after life in common had become impossible, he wished to divorce his wife—whereupon she killed him. The jury acquitted her, and here are some of the good reasons the accused proffered: "One does not regret a man who, at the decline of his life, fails to complete the good deed he has begun. What I regret is the fact that I had to kill him because he had left me. I also killed him because he had asked for a divorce, because he has covered me with shame and at the same time defiled his own name. I, a divorcée? never! So, there was only one solution left."* The influence of feminism and of theatrical eloquence is clearly seen in the novel and in the press, all in favor of the prostitute. The victim was infected by similar theories, he had written to his wife: "I have taken you as Fantine of *Les Miserables* and I believed in your rehabilitation." This good man, instead of paying attention to Victor Hugo, Dumas Fils and other eulogists of the fallen woman, would have done better to marry a decent girl; and certainly his fault of giving credence to such empty declamations deserved punishment. However, the death penalty was perhaps a little too harsh, and moreover, the manner how and by whom it was administered is an affront to justice. It would seem to anyone not completely intoxicated with "humanitarian" doctrines that those good, sentimental and feminist panel members should have doubted somewhat the theory according to which he who "fails to complete a good deed he began" deserved to be killed by the person who had benefited from such a deed.

The fate of this ill-rewarded *humanitarian* reflects the fate that befell the humanitarian French aristocracy at the time of the revolution. It reflects also the fate that is in store for our bourgeoisie, which will have to expiate, by loss of property if not by the guillotine, the fault of "not having completed the good deed" to which it is now so dedicated, at least in words, while it endeavors to relieve, to rehabilitate and glorify the wretched and degenerate, the vicious and delinquent. "As long as the sun shall shine upon man's misfortunes, the sheep will be eaten by the wolf."* All that is left is, for those who know and can, to avoid becoming sheep.

At the banquet of the republican Committee of Commerce and Industry, which took place on June 22, 1900, Millerand[2] began with the usual phrases, and declared that he was moved by the acknowledgment "of the efforts which I attempted toward some progress along the road of *social justice,* which road the republic

must forever follow without fail, and toward the work of *social rehabilitation,* which means to bend in compassion toward the most unfortunate and to try to give them more justice and well-being." And then he addressed those bourgeoisie in friendly tones, speaking about an alliance: "Our ministry has shown the necessity of an alliance between the bourgeoisie and the workers, and we must prove that we are proud of it." Not one among those present remembered the old fable:

Nunquam est fidelis cum potente societas,[3] and dared answer the citizen, "the comrade," and minister: "After we shall have helped you defeat the nationalists, you will act like the lion in the fable and take everything":

Sic totam praedam sola improbitas abstulit.[4] "You have already made a beginning. You call us allies but you permit that we be robbed with impunity. For good measure, your friend Jaurès,[5] whom you have made a member of the Labor Department, proposes that, if the majority of the workers wish to strike, the minority must be constrained by the police to obey, and management is forbidden to keep part of the striking labor at work or to hire others not involved in the strike." There were many industrialists present, and not one had the courage even to whisper. People with so little spirit do not rightly deserve any regard. Thinking of them, Millerand could have remembered the words of Tiberius about another degenerated elite: *O homines ad servitutem paratos.*[6]

---

[2] Alexandre Millerand (1859–1943), at that time Socialist minister of commerce, later minister of war, and President of France, 1920–1924—Ed.

[3] "An alliance with a powerful man is never safe," from a fable by Phaedrus—Ed.

[4] "Thus dishonesty took all the spoils"—Ed.

[5] Jean Jaurès, professor of philosophy and parliamentary leader of the Socialist party, assassinated July 1914—Ed.

[6] "O men, how you prepare yourselves for slavery," Tiberius according to Tacitus—Ed.

It is pitiful to observe how all the parties flatter and adulate the people. Even a man like Galliffet[7] proclaims, in the French Parlement, that he is a socialist! They all prostrate themselves at the feet of the new sovereign and debase themselves before him.

It is, in part, from this steadily growing weakness of the bourgeoisie that the new religious fervor which pervades that class stems. Hence this weakness is also one of the many causes of the present religious crisis. It has often been said that the devil, when he grows old, becomes a monk; often a courtesan on whom the years begin to weigh gives up her wicked ways and turns into a bigot. The case of the bourgeoisie is not at all similar, for though it has become bigoted, it has not given up its wicked ways.

The humanitarian sentiments and the sensibility which it exhibits are inflated, artificial, and false. Admittedly, prostitutes, thieves, and murderers deserve compassion, but is not an honest mother of a family, is not a man of honor and integrity equally worthy? It is good and noble to enter into the sufferings of the poor of today and try to alleviate them. But the sufferings of tomorrow's poor, those who live in ease today and are to be despoiled and reduced to misery, are they made of different stuff? In reality the bourgeoisie of today does not look to the future; it exploits the present and thereafter—the deluge. Its sensibility gives vent in words, often concealing base profits. The weak are usually also vile; they practice skillful larceny but do not venture to commit armed robbery.

---

[7] General Marquis de Galliffet (1830–1909) crushed the uprising of the Paris Commune in 1871, became a symbol of the separation between soldier and state when in 1875 he ordered his officers to stay out of politics, served as minister of war from 1899 to 1900 in the same cabinet as Millerand, and contributed to the revision of the Dreyfus case—Ed.

Elites in a stage of decline generally display humanitarian sentiments and great kindness; but this kindness, provided it is not imply weakness, is more seeming than real. Seneca was a perfect stoic, but he possessed great riches, splendid palaces, innumerable slaves. The French noblemen who applauded Rousseau knew how to make their "fermiers" pay; and the new love of virtue dissipating in orgies with whores, the money extorted from the peasants, who were starving to death. Today in France a landowner collects, thanks to the duties on grain and cattle, thousands of lire from his fellow citizens; he donates a hundred lire or a little more to a "People's University," and with his purse thus fattened, appeases his conscience and hopes in addition, to be elected at the polls. To be moved with compassion for the poor and destitute in the midst of luxuries agreeably stimulates the senses. Many are landowners today and socialists in the future, and so they feed from two mangers at a time. That future is so far away, who knows when it will come! In the meantime it is sweet to enjoy one's wealth and to discuss equality, to pick up friendships, public offices, sometimes also to find good opportunities for making money, and to pay with words and future promises. There is always a profit to gain by bartering a sure asset for a promissory note signed for so long and uncertain a term.

The sums which the ruling class appropriates illicitly, thanks to protective duties, from premiums on navigation, on sugar, and many related products, to enterprises subsidized by the State, the syndicates, trusts, etc., are enormous and certainly comparable to the sums which, during other periods, were extorted by other ruling classes. The only advantage for the nation is the fact that the method of clipping the sheep has been perfected; hence, for the same amount of extorted wealth the amount squandered is smaller. The feudal lord who robbed the wayfarers obstructed the expansion of commerce; he stole a few soldi and indirectly destroyed several lire; his successor, who benefits from protective duties, illicitly appropriates a large amount of wealth but indirectly destroys less.

Our ruling class is insatiable; as its power wanes, its fraudulent practices increase. Every day in France, in Italy, in Germany, in America, it demands new tightenings of duties, new provisions to safeguard trade, new obstacles to commerce under the pretext of sanitary provisions, new subsidies of every kind. In Italy, under Depretis,[8] the government used to send soldiers to mow the fields of landowners who refused to pay the wages requested by free mowers; today this fine practice is being renewed. It seems the feudal corvées are on their way back. The soldiers, instead of being used solely for the defense of the country, serve the landowners to keep down wages that would otherwise be fixed by free competition.

Such is the method of despoiling the poor, applied by our foremost "humanitarians." Congresses against tuberculosis are fine, but it would be even better not to steal the bread from those who starve and it would also be preferable, either to be a little less "humanitarian," or to respect the property of others a little more.

There is not the least sign to indicate that the dominant class is about to abandon the bad road, and it is to be assumed that it will continue to tread it until the days of final catastrophe. This could already be seen in France as regards the old aristocracy. To the very eve of the revolution they were besieging that unfortunate Louis XVI, clamoring for money.* In Italy one could see, under Depretis, systematically ordered robbery and pillage. From the elector to the elected, all were selling and buying each other. The tightening of protectionism in 1887 was used as a means to auction off to the highest bidder the right to impose private levies on the citizens; others made their profits on railroads, banks, steel mills, and the merchant marine. The entire ruling class crowded around the government demanding, with great outcries, at least a bone to nibble on. It was then that the bad seed was sown; its fruits were the tears and the blood of May 1898,[9] and even bitterer fruits may ripen in the future. The unlawful appropriations of the ruling class were countered by the violence of the people, subdued but not conquered by unjust repression. I say unjust, because it was intended, not to protect order and property, but to defend privileges, to perpetuate robbery, and to render possible such scandalous acts as the Notarbartolo trial.[10]

We wish to caution the reader that where we speak of the diminishing

---

[8] Augostino Depretis, Italian prime minister from 1876 to 1879, liberalized trade, reorganized higher education, and banned religious ceremonies and processions outside of the churches — Ed.

[9] The colonial policy of Depretis' successor, Francesco Crispi — a left-wing opportunist who had to resign in 1896 when the Italian army was defeated in Ethiopia — caused a domestic depression aggravated by the Spanish-American War. Bread riots broke out in Rome, Parma, Florence, and Milan where troops mistook beggars before a convent for revolutionary soldiers and killed eighty people. The commanding general was decorated, universities closed, village banks and labor unions dissolved, newspapers and some 3000 Catholic organizations suppressed, and order restored by martial law — Ed.

[10] In 1902 a Sicilian deputy was sentenced to thirty years in prison for having instigated in 1895 the murder of Senator Emanuele Notarbartolo, former mayor of Palermo, and director of the Bank of Sicily, who had fought corruption in finance and politics. According to C. Seton-Watson, *Italy from Liberalism to Fascism* (London, 1967), p. 309, "A sensation was caused by the evidence which emerged during the trial of the Mafia's power to terrorise, obstruct justice and penetrate the state machine" — Ed.

strength of the dominant class, we by no means refer to a decrease in violence; it even occurs very frequently that the weak are precisely those who are also violent. None is more cruel and violent than the coward. Strength and violence are two entirely different concepts. Trajan was strong and not violent; Nero was violent but not strong.

If, as is probable, the contrast between the evil deeds, which are forever increasing, and the spirit, courage, and strength, which are progressively declining, should become more acute, the end can only be a violent catastrophe, which will restore the equilibrium that has been so gravely disturbed.

The most pilloried point in the OSWALD SPENGLER controversy was his opinion that the West had entered its "period of the contending states." Spengler still held this view in his last published words, a cabled reply to an American poll, "Is World Peace Possible?" (*Cosmopolitan,* January 1936). Spengler's prognosis provoked public opinion during a decade which began with a peace treaty (1919) to "end all wars" and make the world "safe for democracy" and which was climaxed by the Kellogg pact (1928) in which all nations renounced war. The American philosopher John Dewey expected that the anniversaries of the Kellogg pact would replace Christmas. This selection also includes Spengler's depiction of the press as a mobilizer of modern war and an instrument of Caesarism.*

Oswald Spengler

The Period of the Contending States

With the beginning of the twentieth century Parliamentarism (even English) is tending rapidly towards taking up itself the role that it once assigned to the kingship. It is becoming an impressive spectacle for the multitude of the Orthodox, while the centre of gravity of big policy, already *de jure* transferred from the Crown to the people's representatives, is passing *de facto* from the latter to unofficial groups and the will of unofficial personages. The World War [I] almost completed this development. There is no way back to the old parliamentarism from the domination of Lloyd George and the Napoleonism of the French milita-

rists. And for America, hitherto lying apart and self-contained, rather a region than a State, the parallelism of President and Congress which she derived from a theory of Montesquieu has, with her entry into world politics, become untenable, and must in times of real danger make way for formless powers such as those with which Mexico and South America have long been familiar.

With this enters the age of gigantic conflicts, in which we find ourselves today. It is the *transition from Napoleonism to Caesarism,* a general phase of evolution, which occupies at least two centuries and can be shown to exist in all the Cul-

*From *The Decline of the West* (abridged edition), by Oswald Spengler. Arthur Helps, editor of English abridgment, from the translation of Charles Francis Atkinson. © Copyright 1962 by Alfred A. Knopf, Inc. Abridged trans. © Allen & Unwin Ltd. 1961. Reprinted by permission of Alfred A. Knopf, Inc. Pp. 374–377. Second part from *The Decline of the West,* Vol. II, by Oswald Spengler, trans. by Charles Francis Atkinson. Copyright 1928 and renewed 1956 by Alfred A. Knopf, Inc. Reprinted by permission of the publisher. Pp. 460–464.

tures. The Chinese call it Shan-Kwo, the "period of the Contending States."

For us this time of Contending States began with Napoleon and his violent-arbitrary government by order. He was the first in our world to make effective the notion of a military and at the same time popular world-domination—something altogether different from the Empire of Charles V and even the British Colonial Empire of his own day. If the nineteenth century was relatively poor in great wars—and revolutions—and overcame its worst crises diplomatically by means of congresses, this has been due precisely to the continuous and terrific war-preparedness which has made disputants, fearful at the eleventh hour of the consequences, postpone the definitive decision again and again, and led to the substitution of chess-moves for war. For this is the century of gigantic permanent armies and universal compulsory service. We ourselves are too near to it to see it under this terrifying aspect. In all world-history there is no parallel. Ever since Napoleon, hundreds of thousands, and latterly millions, of men have stood ready to march, and mighty fleets renewed every ten years have filled the harbours. It is a war without war, a war of over-bidding in equipment and preparedness, a war of figures and tempo and technics, and the diplomatic dealings have been not of court with court, but of headquarters with headquarters. The longer the discharge was delayed, the more huge became the means and the more intolerable the tension. This is the Faustian, the dynamic, form of "the Contending States" during the first century of that period, but it ended with the explosion of the World War. For the demand of these four years has been altogether too much for the principle of universal service—child of the French Revolution,

revolutionary through and through, as it is in this form—and all tactical methods evolved from it. The place of the permanent armies as we know them will gradually be taken by professional forces of volunteer war-keen soldiers; and from millions we shall revert to hundreds of thousands. But *ipso facto* this second century will be one of *actually* Contending States. *These* armies are not substitutes for war—they are *for* war, and they want war. Within two generations it will be their will that prevails over that of all the comfortables put together. In these wars of theirs for the heritage of the whole world, continents will be staked, India, China, South Africa, Russia, Islam, called out, new technics and tactics played and counterplayed. The great cosmopolitan foci of power will dispose at their pleasure of smaller states—their territory, their economy and their men alike—all that is now merely province, passive object, means to end, and its destinies are without importance to the great march of things. We ourselves, in a very few years, have learned to take little or no notice of events that before the War would have horrified the world; who today seriously thinks about the millions that perish in Russia?

Again and again between these catastrophes of blood and terror the cry rises up for reconciliation of the peoples and for peace on earth. It is but the background and the echo of the grand happening, but, as such, so necessary that we have to assume its existence even if, as in Hyksos Egypt, in Baghdad and Byzantium, no tradition tells of it. Esteem as we may the wish towards all this, we must have the courage to face facts as they are—that is the hallmark of men of race-quality and it is by the being of these men that *alone* history is. Life if it would be great, is hard; it lets choose *only* between victory and ruin, not between war and peace, and to the victory belong the sacrifices of victory. For that which shuffles querulously and jealously by the side of the events is only literature—written or thought or lived literature—mere truths that lose themselves in the moving crush of facts. History has never deigned to take notice of these propositions. In the Chinese world Hiang-Sui tried, as early as 535, to found a peace league. In the period of the Contending States, imperialism *(Lien-heng)* was opposed by the League of Nations idea *(Hoh-tsung)*, particularly in the southern regions, but it was foredoomed like every half-measure that steps into the path of a whole, and it had vanished even before the victory of the North. But both tendencies alike rejected the political taste of the Taoists, who, in those fearful centuries, elected for intellectual self-disarmament, thereby reducing themselves to the level of mere material to be used up by others and for others in the grand decisions. Even Roman politics—deliberately improvident as the Classical spirit was in all other respects—at least made one attempt to bring the whole world into one system of equal co-ordinated forces which should do away with all necessity for further wars—that is, when at the fall of Hannibal Rome forwent the chance of incorporating the East. But reluctance was useless; the party of the younger Scipio went over to frank Imperialism in order to make an end of chaos, although its clear-sighted leader foresaw therein the doom of his city, which possessed (and in a high degree) the native Classical incapacity for organizing anything whatever. The way from Alexander to Caesar is unambiguous and unavoidable, and the strongest nation of any and every Culture, consciously or unconsciously, willing or unwilling, has had to tread it.

From the rigour of these facts there is no refuge. The Hague Conference of 1907 was the prelude of the World War; the Washington Conference of 1921 will have been that of other wars. The history of these times is no longer an intellectual match of wits in elegant forms for pluses and minuses, from which either side can withdraw when it pleases. The alternatives now are to stand fast or to go under—there is no middle course. . . .

Gunpowder and printing belong together—both discovered at the culmination of the Gothic, both arising out of Germanic technical thought—as *the two* grand means of Faustian distance-tactics. The Reformation in the beginning of the Late period witnessed the first flysheets and the first field-guns, the French Revolution in the beginning of the Civilization witnessed the first tempest of pamphlets of the autumn of 1788 and the first mass-fire of artillery at Valmy. But with this the printed word, produced in vast quantity and distributed over enormous areas, became an uncanny weapon in the hands of him who knew how to use it. In France it was still in 1788 a matter of expressing private convictions, but England was already past that, and deliberately seeking to produce impressions on the reader. The war of articles, flysheets, spurious memoirs, that was waged from London on French soil against Napoleon is the first great example. The scattered sheets of the Age of Enlightenment transformed themselves into "the Press"—a term of most significant anonymity. Now the *press campaign* appears as the prolongation—or the preparation—of war by other means, and in the course of the nineteenth century the strategy of outpose fights, feints, surprises, assaults, is developed to such a degree that a war may be lost ere the first shot is fired—because the Press has won it meantime.

To-day we live so cowed under the

bombardment of this intellectual artillery that hardly anyone can attain to the inward detachment that is required for a clear view of the monstrous drama. The will-to-power operating under a pure democratic disguise has finished off its masterpiece so well that the object's sense of freedom is actually flattered by the most thorough-going enslavement that has ever existed. The liberal bourgeois mind is *proud* of the abolition of censorship, the last restraint, while the dictator of the press—Northcliffe![1]—keeps the slave-gang of his readers under the whip of his leading articles, telegrams, and pictures. *Democracy has by its newspaper completely expelled the book from the mental life of the people.* The book-world, with its profusion of standpoints that compelled thought to select and criticize, is now a real possession only for a few. The people reads the *one* paper, "its" paper, which forces itself through the front doors by millions daily, spell-binds the intellect from morning to night, drives the book into oblivion by its more engaging layout, and if one or another specimen of a book does emerge into visibility, forestalls and eliminates its possible effects by "reviewing" it.

What is truth? For the multitude, that which it continually reads and hears. A forlorn little drop may settle somewhere and collect grounds on which to determine "the truth"—but what it obtains is just *its* truth. The other, the public truth of the moment, which alone matters for effects and successes in the fact-world, is to-day a product of the Press. What the Press wills, is true. Its commanders evoke, transform, interchange truths. Three weeks of press work, and the truth is acknowledged by everybody. Its bases are irrefutable for just so long as money is

[1] British press lord (1865–1922) who pioneered "illustrated" newscasting before the advent of radio and television—Ed.

available to maintain them intact. The Classical rhetoric, too, was designed for effect and not content—as Shakespeare brilliantly demonstrates in Antony's funeral oration—but it did limit itself to the bodily audience and the moment. What the dynamism of our Press wants is *permanent* effectiveness. It must keep men's minds continuously under its influence. Its arguments are overthrown as soon as the advantage of financial power passes over to the counter-arguments and brings these still oftener to men's eyes and ears. At that moment the needle of public opinion swings round to the stronger pole. Everybody convinces himself at once of the new truth, and regards himself awakened out of error.

With the political press is bound up the need of universal school-education, which in the Classical world was completely lacking. In this demand there is an element—quite unconscious—of desiring to shepherd the masses, as the object of party politics, into the newspaper's power-area. The idealist of the early democracy regarded popular education, without *arrière pensée* [ulterior motives], as enlightenment pure and simple, and even to-day one finds here and there weak heads that become enthusiastic on the Freedom of the Press—but it is precisely this that smooths the path for the coming Caesars of the world-press. Those who have learnt to read succumb to their power, and the visionary self-determination of Late democracy issues in a thorough-going determination of the people by the powers whom the printed word obeys.

In the contests of to-day tactics consists in depriving the opponent of this weapon. In the unsophisticated infancy of its power the newspaper suffered from official censorship which the champions of tradition wielded in self-defence, and the bourgeoisie cried out that the freedom of the spirit was in danger. Now the multitude placidly goes its way; it has definitively won for itself this freedom. But in the background, unseen, the new forces are fighting one another by buying the press. Without the reader's observing it, the paper, *and himself with it,* changes masters. Here also money triumphs and forces the free spirits into its service. No tamer has his animals more under his power. Unleash the people as reader-mass and it will storm through the streets and hurl itself upon the target indicated, terrifying and breaking windows; a hint to the press-staff and it will become quiet and go home. The Press to-day is an army with carefully organized arms and branches, with journalists as officers, and readers as soldiers. But here, as in every army, the soldier obeys blindly, and war-aims and operation-plans change without his knowledge. The reader neither knows, nor is allowed to know, the purposes for which he is used, nor even the rôle that he is to play. A more appalling caricature of freedom of thought cannot be imagined. Formerly a man did not dare to think freely. Now he dares, but cannot; his will to think is only a willingness to think to order, and this is what he feels as *his* liberty.

And the other side of this belated freedom—it is permitted to everyone to say what he pleases, *but* the Press is free to take notice of what he says or not. It can condemn any "truth" to death simply by not undertaking its communication to the world—a terrible consorship of silence, which is all the more potent in that the masses of newspaper readers are absolutely unaware that it exists. Here, as ever in the birth-pangs of Caesarism, emerges a trait of the buried springtime. The arc of happening is about to close on itself. Just as in the concrete and steel buildings the expression-will of early

Gothic once more bursts forth, but cold, controlled, and Civilized, so the iron will of the Gothic Church to power over souls reappears as—the "freedom of democracy." The age of the "book" is flanked on either hand by that of the sermon and that of the newspaper. Books are a personal expression, sermon and newspaper obey an impersonal *purpose.* The years of Scholasticism afford the only example in world-history of an intellectual discipline that was applied universally and permitted no writing, no speech, no thought to come forth that contradicted the *willed* unity. This is spiritual dynamics. Classical, Indian, or Chinese mankind would have been horrified at this spectacle. But the same things recur, and as a *necessary* result of the European-American liberalism—"the despotism of freedom against tyranny," as Robespierre put it. In lieu of stake and faggots there is the great silence. The dictature of party leaders supports itself upon that of the Press. The competitors strive by means of money to detach readers—nay, peoples—*en masse* from the hostile allegiance and to bring them under their own mind-training. And all that they learn in this mind-training, is what it is considered that they should know—a higher will puts together the picture of their world for them. There is no need now, as there was for Baroque princes, to impose military-service liability on the subject—one whips their souls with articles, telegrams, and pictures (Northcliffe!) until they *clamour* for weapons and force their leaders into a conflict to which they *willed* to be forced.

This is the end of Democracy. If in the world of truths it is *proof* that decides all, in that of facts it is *success.* Success means that one being triumphs over the others. Life has won through, and the dreams of the world-improvers have turned out to be but the tools of *master*-natures. In the Late Democracy, *race*[2] bursts forth and either makes ideals its slaves or throws them scornfully into the pit. It was so, too, in Egyptian Thebes, in Rome, in China—but in no other Civilization has the will-to-power manifested itself in so inexorable a form as in this of ours. The thought, and consequently the action, of the mass are kept under iron pressure —for which reason, and for which reason only, men are permitted to be readers and voters—that is, in a dual slavery— while the parties become the obedient retinues of a few, and the shadow of coming Caesarism already touches them. As

---

[2] The German noun *Rasse* for "race" has two different meanings that are revealed by its adjectives *rassisch* and *rassig*. *Rassisch* means racial, pertaining to a particular race. Nietzsche and Spengler, however, used *Rasse* (the result of long breeding) in the sense of *rassig* (true to type), such as a Japanese girl with peach skin and black cherry eyes and hair. *Rasse* in the sense of *rassig* is rather a matter of esthetic appreciation than of racial discrimination—Ed.

the English kingship became in the nineteenth century, so parliaments will become in the twentieth, a solemn and empty pageantry. As then sceptre and crown, so now peoples' rights are paraded for the multitude, and all the more punctiliously the less they really signify—it was for this reason that the *cautious* Augustus never let pass an opportunity of emphasizing old and venerated customs of Roman freedom. But the power is migrating even to-day, and correspondingly elections are degenerating for us into the farce that they were in Rome. Money organizes the process in the interests of those who possess it, and election affairs become a preconcerted game that is staged as popular self-determination. If election was originally *revolution in legitimate forms,* it has exhausted those forms, and what takes place is that mankind "elects" its Destiny again by the primitive methods of bloody violence when the politics of money become intolerable.

ALBERT SCHWEITZER (1875–1965) forsook a successful career as professor of Protestant theology at the University of Strasbourg, studied medicine, and in 1913 founded a tropical hospital at Lambaréné in the African republic of Gabon, formerly the French Congo. Schweitzer wished to atone for the white man's sins against the Negro people. In subsequent years, he raised the funds for his medical care by lecture tours, organ recitals, and the publication of scholarly works. His *Philosophy of Civilization* (1923) came into being during World War I in a French internment camp. In 1952 Schweitzer received the Nobel Prize for peace and together with Mahatma Gandhi was widely hailed as a modern saint.*

Albert Schweitzer

The Nature and Restoration
of Civilization

Entering on the question as to what is the real essential nature of civilization, I come to the pronouncement that this is ultimately ethical. I know that in thus stating the problem as a moral one I shall surprise and even disgust the spirit of our times, which is accustomed to move amidst aesthetic, historical and material considerations. I imagine, however, that I am myself enough of an artist and also of an historian to be able to comprehend the aesthetic and historical elements in civilization, and that, as a modern physician and surgeon, I am sufficiently modern to appreciate the glamour of the technical and material attainments of our age.

Notwithstanding this, I have come to the conviction that the aesthetic and the historical elements, and the magnificent extension of our material knowledge and power, do not themselves form the essence of civilization, but that this depends on the mental disposition of the individuals and nations who exist in the world. All other things are merely accompanying circumstances of civilization, which have nothing to do with its real essence.

Creative, artistic, intellectual, and material attainments can only show their full and true effects when the continued existence and development of civilization have been secured by founding civilization itself on a mental disposition which is truly ethical. It is only in his struggle to become ethical that man comes to possess real value as a personality; it is only

*From the author's preface to *The Philosophy of Civilization* by Albert Schweitzer, translated by C. T. Campion, pp. xi–xv. Published by A. & C. Black Ltd, London, and The Macmillan Company, New York. Reprinted by permission.

under the influence of ethical convictions that the various relations of human society are formed in such a way that individuals and people can develop in an ideal manner. If the ethical foundation is lacking, then civilization collapses, even when in other directions creative and intellectual forces of the strongest nature are at work.

This moral conception of civilization, which makes me almost a stranger amidst the intellectual life of my time, I express clearly and unhesitatingly, in order to arouse amongst my contemporaries reflection as to what civilization really is. We shall not succeed in re-establishing our civilization on an enduring basis until we rid ourselves completely of the superficial concept of civilization which now holds us in thrall, and give ourselves up again to the ethical view which obtained in the eighteenth century.

The second point which I desire should obtain currency is that of the connection between civilization and our theory of the universe. At the present time no regard is paid to this connection. In fact, the period in which we are living altogether misses the significance of having a theory of the universe. It is the common conviction nowadays, of educated and uneducated alike, that humanity will progress quite satisfactorily without any theory of the universe at all.

The real fact is that all human progress depends on progress in its theory of the universe, whilst, conversely, decadence is conditioned by a similar decadence in this theory. Our loss of real civilization is due to our lack of a theory of the universe.

Only as we again succeed in attaining a strong and worthy theory of the universe, and find in it strong and worthy convictions, shall we again become capable of producing a new civilization. It is this

apparently abstract and paradoxical truth of which I proclaim myself the champion.

Civilization, put quite simply, consists in our giving ourselves, as human beings, to the effort to attain the perfecting of the human race and the actualization of progress of every sort in the circumstances of humanity and of the objective world. This mental attitude, however, involves a double predisposition: firstly, we must be prepared to act affirmatively toward the world and life; secondly, we must become ethical.

Only when we are able to attribute a real meaning to the world and to life shall we be able also to give ourselves to such action as will produce results of real value. As long as we look on our existence in the world as meaningless, there is no point whatever in desiring to effect anything in the world. We become workers for that universal spiritual and material progress which we call civilization only in so far as we affirm that the world and life possess some sort of meaning, or, which is the same thing, only in so far as we think optimistically.

Civilization originates when men become inspired by a strong and clear determination to attain progress, and consecrate themselves, as a result of this determination, to the service of life and of the world. It is only in ethics that we can find the driving force for such action, transcending, as it does, the limits of our own existence.

Nothing of real value in the world is ever accomplished without enthusiasm and self-sacrifice.

But it is impossible to convince men of the truth of world- and life-affirmation and of the real value of ethics by mere declamation. The affirmative and ethical mentality which characterizes these beliefs must originate in man himself as the result of an inner spiritual relation to the world. Only then will they accompany him as strong, clear, and constant convictions, and condition his every thought and action.

To put it in another way: World- and life-affirmation must be the products of thought about the world and life. Only as the majority of individuals attain to this result of thought and continue under its influence will a true and enduring civilization make progress in the world. Should the mental disposition toward world- and life-affirmation and toward ethics begin to wane, or become dim and obscured, we shall be incapable of working for true civilization, nay, more, we shall be unable even to form a correct concept of what such civilization ought to be.

And this is the fate which has befallen us. We are bereft of any theory of the universe. Therefore, instead of being inspired by a profound and powerful spirit of affirmation of the world and of life, we allow ourselves, both as individuals and as nations, to be driven hither and thither by a type of such affirmation which is both confused and superficial. Instead of adopting a determined ethical attitude, we exist in an atmosphere of mere ethical phrases or declare ourselves ethical sceptics.

How is it that we have got into this state of lacking a theory of the universe? It is because hitherto the world- and life-affirming and ethical theory of the universe had no convincing and permanent foundation in thought. We thought again and again that we had found such a basis for it; but it lost power again and again without our being aware that it was doing so, until, finally, we have been obliged, for more than a generation past, to resign ourselves more and more to a complete lack of any world-theory at all.

Thus, in this introductory part of my work, I proclaim two truths and conclude with a great note of interrogation. The truths are the following: The basic ethical character of civilization, and the connection between civilization and our theories of the universe. The question with which I conclude is this: Is it at all possible to find a real and permanent foundation in thought for a theory of the universe which shall be both ethical and affirmative of the world and of life?

The future of civilization depends on our overcoming the meaninglessness and hopelessness which characterize the thoughts and convictions of men to-day, and reaching a state of fresh hope and fresh determination. We shall be capable of this, however, only when the majority of individuals discover for themselves both an ethic and a profound and steadfast attitude of world- and life-affirmation, in a theory of the universe at once convincing and based on reflection.

Without such a general spiritual experience there is no possibility of holding our world back from the ruin and disintegration toward which it is being hastened. It is our duty then to rouse ourselves to fresh reflection about the world and life.

... The root-idea of my theory of the universe is that my relation to my own being and to the objective world is determined by reverence for life. This reverence for life is given as an element of my will-to-live, and becomes clearly conscious of itself as I reflect about my life and about the world. In the mental attitude of reverence for life which should characterize my contact with all forms of life, both ethics and world- and life-affirmation are involved. It is not any kind of insight into the essential nature of the world which determines my relation to my own existence and to the existence which I encounter in the world, but rather only and solely my own will-to-live which has developed the power of reflection about itself and the world.

The theory of the universe characterized by reverence for life is a type of mysticism arrived at by self-consistent thought when persisted in to its ultimate conclusion. Surrendering himself to the guidance of this mysticism, man finds a meaning for his life in that he strives to accomplish his own spiritual and ethical self-fulfilment, and, simultaneously and in the same act, helps forward all the processes of spiritual and material progress which have to be actualized in the world.

I do not know how many, or how few, will allow themselves to be persuaded to travel with me on the road indicated above. What I desire above all things— and this is the crux of the whole affair— is that we should all recognize fully that our present entire lack of any theory of the universe is the ultimate source of all the catastrophes and misery of our times, and that we should work together for a theory of the universe and of life, in order that thus we may arrive at a mental disposition which shall make us really and truly civilized men.

In his *Social Philosophies* (1950), PITIRIM A. SOROKIN charged Schweitzer with proposing a remedy for our civilizational decay, which itself was the root of the evil. Here, he outlines a program for a "complete change of the contemporary mentality, a fundamental transformation of our system of values, and the profoundest modification of our conduct toward other men, cultural values, and the world at large." Sorokin puts teeth into his proposal by pointing out that failure to reform peacefully and voluntarily has always resulted in violent change by the force of circumstance.*

Pitirim A. Sorokin

The Roots and the Cure of the Crisis

It is now in order to ask: How has this tragic crisis come about? What are its roots and reasons? Why has contemporary man—so successful in his scientific and technological achievements—not prevented the disintegration of his sensate culture and of his own degradation and tragedy?

Most of the current answers hardly scratch the surface of the problem. They view it as a mere maladjustment of purely economic, or political, or technological, or biological nature. The maladjustment is regarded as something incidental, not inherent in the nature of modern sensate culture. Accordingly, for the elimination of the evil, they prescribe with perfect confidence either an economic readjustment—in money and banking, in prices and wages, in social security and insurance against unemployment, old age, or disease, even to the elimination of private property; or else a modification of the political machinery—from a reconstruction of the League of Nations, a monarchy or a republic, a democracy, or a totalitarian state, to a reform of the civil service or the system of political parties.

Other doctors see salvation in a mild religious therapy: making the churches more comfortable, the services more attractive, and the sermons more entertaining. Still others believe in the magic power of education and expect marvels from changing here and there the curricula of schools; from an increase of Bachelors, Masters, and Doctors of all sciences

*From the book *The Crisis of Our Age* by Pitirim A. Sorokin. Copyright, 1941, by E. P. Dutton & Co., Inc. Renewal, ©, 1969 by Helen P. Sorokin. Reprinted by permission of the publishers. Pp. 308–326.

real and imaginary; from "educational talks" in clubs, forums, town halls, by radio and television, especially of the type of the "Professor Quiz" and the "Information, Please" programs; finally, from the continuous reading of daily papers and magazines, Digests, and Digests of Digests. There are also those doctors who see the root of the evil in a biological deterioration, wrong heredity, wrong race, negative selection, and other biological factors. Respectively they put great faith in such measures as birth-control, the increasing consumption of vitamins, the sterilization of the socially unfit, racial purity, and the like. Finally, some of the experts find the source of the trouble in sunspots, climate and misbehavior of the cosmic factors; these console us, however, by assuring us that the sun soon will be less spotty, the climate less naughty, and that everything will soon be all right.

There is no doubt that some of these measures, when properly applied, can produce some minor improvements. But there is also no doubt that none of these reaches the source of the virus. Not touching the source, they cannot eliminate the disease.

The reason for such a statement is quite inductive. All these palliative measures, without any exception whatsoever, have been applied several times. And yet they neither prevented, nor stopped, nor eliminated the crisis. Not infrequently some of them only aggravated the situation. So much for all the economic, political, educational, and other prescriptions. As for the "sunspot" and biological theories, no sunspot or purely climatic theory has been able to account for the historical destinies of any of the great cultures of the past. Still less do they account for the small and great "swings" in the rise of a sensate culture that has lasted for several

centuries—regardless of cycles of climate, sunspots, or any other cosmic conditions. Still less do they account for the present crisis. Generally, incessant change of socio-cultural life has very little to do with these factors. Biologically, recent generations appear to be more healthy than past ones: the stature of the present generation has increased; its duration of life has increased also; its diseases have diminished. Biologically we are as good as any previous generation. In spite of all the alarm raised by eugenists, racialists, and hereditarists, the trouble does not lie in biological conditions.

For these reasons one can seriously doubt the adequacy of these diagnoses as well as their remedies. Their error consists in looking for the source of the tragedy in the wrong place, in underestimation of the character of the disease, and especially in viewing it as something incidental, not inherent in the very nature of modern overripe sensate culture. In fact, the roots of the tragedy lie infinitely deeper. They are immanent, go far back, and are inherent in sensate culture. The same forces that determined the growth of its magnificent achievements made unavoidable the growth of the cancer of its disintegration and crisis. The price and the Nemesis of sensate culture is this *alter ego,* the Siamese twin of its growth and magnificence.

We have seen that modern sensate culture[1] emerged with a major belief that true reality and true value were mainly or exclusively sensory. Anything that was supersensory was either doubtful

---

[1] *Sensate* culture, according to Sorokin, recognizes no reality, and no source of values beyond that which can be seen, heard, smelled, touched, and tasted. By contrast, the *ideational* culture of the Middle Ages used the Christian creed as criterion of truth and downgraded the testimony of the senses. *Idealistic* culture is "a synthesis of both, made by our reason."—Ed.

as a reality or fictitious as a value. It either did not exist or, being unperceivable by the senses, amounted to the nonexistent. Respectively, the organs of senses, with the secondary help of human reason, were made the main arbiter of the true and false, of the real and unreal, and of the valuable and valueless. Any charismatic-supersensory and superrational revelation, any mystic experience, any truth of faith, began to be denied, as a valid experience, a valid truth, and a genuine value. *The major premise of the sensory nature of the true reality and value is the root from which developed the tree of our sensate culture with its splendid as well as its poisonous fruit.* Its first positive fruit is an *unprecedented development of the natural sciences and technological inventions.* The first poisonous fruit is a *fatal narrowing of the realm of true reality and true value.*

Since true reality and true value were thought to be sensory, anything that was supersensory, from conception of God to the mind of man, anything that was nonmaterial, that could not in the way of daily experience be seen, heard, tasted, touched, or smelled, had to be declared unreal, nonexistent, and of no value. And that is exactly what has happened.

The rude and imperfect human organs of sense were made the supreme arbiter of what was real and what was not, what was value and what was not. As a result, the infinity of the true reality was impoverished and reduced to only one of its aspects—that which our organs of the senses could detect at a given time; all its other aspects which human reason and intuition can comprehend, especially the rare charismatic experience of the few elect, were discarded as nonexistent.

For the same reason, an identical degradation and shortsighted circumscription has affected the world of values generally, and the value of man and his culture particularly. Man himself and all his values were declared to be real only in so far as they were sensory; anything that was in man or in his culture which was imperceptible to the senses of the rank and file of human beings was declared a doubtful or fictitious pseudo-value. In this way man was reduced mainly to anatomy and physiology. Even as the possessor of nonmaterial mind and thought, of consciousness, and of conscience, he was often questioned and denied. In this manner the major premise clipped the wings of man with which he could soar to the vision of more sublime values and the less coarse aspects of reality.

Once the culture entered this path, it had to move along it, toward a greater and greater sensorization of the world of reality and of value. This path led inevitably to the growth of materialism, because nothing can be more sensory than matter; to a more radical mechanisticism, because nothing can be simpler than mechanical motion; to growing hedonism, utilitariansim, and sensuality in the world of the values, because only sensory pleasure and pain, sensory utility and disutility are real from this standpoint. Hence there has been a growth of mechanistic materialism, flat empiricism, superficial positivism, and vulgar utilitarianism bound up with the growth of modern culture.

Man himself and his evaluation of himself could not escape the same trend.

Man as a bearer of the divine ray in the sensory world, as an incarnation of the charismatic grace, was declared a superstitious delusion. His reality and value was reduced to his biological organism, with all its imperfections. No wonder, therefore, that such a conception led to the previously described degradation of man both as a reality and as a value. Certainly there is nothing sacred in an imperfect human organism. In many respects it is more defective than the organisms of other species of creatures. If the value-reality of man is no more and no less than his organism, it is only consistent that he be treated just as other organisms are treated. If he is useful for a given moment, we can care for him, as we care for cows and horses. If he is unserviceable, we can eliminate him, as we eliminate snakes and mosquitoes, parasites and old animals.

This is exactly the treatment man generally gets now especially in those groups where this equation between man and organism is taken most literally. Man as a man has no value whatsoever for most sensate groups at the present time. They do not recognize any charismatic value of man; therefore they treat him exactly as we treat other organisms. Only in so far as man is a Communist or a Nazi, or "New Dealer" or "Old Dealer," or at least, in so far as he obeys and serves the rules of the dominant faction, can he exist, without being deprived of the elementary conditions of decent living. If his "color" is different from the faction's "color," then cold-bloodedly, with scientific efficiency, he is crushed, liquidated, banished, and becomes a nonentity or a negative value. This equation manifests itself in such contemporary phenomena as war, revolutions, crimes, and other forms of brutality discussed earlier. Such a practice is but a logical consequence of the major premise of contemporary culture. These evils are its poisonous growths quite as much as science and technology are its marvelous fruits. Both spring from the same root of the limitation of true reality and value to the reality of the senses.

From the same root have grown the

other forms of degradation of man, atomization of values, and disintegration of culture surveyed before: in art and philosophy, in law and ethics, and so on. They are largely the consequence of the major premise for the same reasons. The same root is responsible for present-day society as an enormous number of armed camps, that by direct or indirect application of force and fraud try each to defeat the others. Relationships of employers and employees, bankers and labor unions, of social classes to one another, of rich and poor, of educated and noneducated, of privileged and underprivileged, of political parties, occupational groups, and finally, of nations, are at the present time in an incessant war, controlled mainly by the rude force and trickery which a given group has. He who has greater force triumphs, while the weaker party is pitilessly trampled on and crushed. Such is the root of the crisis of our sensate culture.

Since the Western culture is entering the transitional period from its sensate supersystem into either an ideational or an idealistic phase; and since such epoch-making transitions have hitherto been the period of the tragic *dies irae, dies illa,*[2] the greatest task of our time evidently consists, if not in averting tragedy —which is hardly possible—then, at least, in making the transition as painless as possible. What means and ways can help in this task? We leave without further discussion the numerous subsidiary means, like the political, economic, educational, genetic, and other prescriptions which, if they are sound, may somewhat alleviate the tragedy but can in no way prevent it or serve as the "way out" from

---

[2] "Day of reckoning," the opening line of a thirteenth-century Latin hymn by Thomas of Celano— Ed.

it. The most important means evidently consists in the correction of the fatal mistake of the sensate phase and in a concerted preparation for the inevitable mental and moral and socio-cultural revolution of Western society. The first step in this direction consists in *as wide, as deep, and as prompt realization as possible of the extraordinary character of the contemporary crisis of our culture and society.* It is high time to realize that this is not one of the ordinary crises which happen almost every decade, but one of the greatest transitions in human history from one of its main forms of culture to another. An adequate realization of the immense magnitude of the change now upon us is a necessary condition for determining the adequacy of measures and means to alleviate the magnitude of the pending catastrophe. He is a poor doctor who treats dangerous pneumonia as a slight cold. Similarly, nothing but harm can ensue from the prevalent treatment of the present crisis as a slight and ordinary maladjustment. Such a blundering diagnosis must be forgotten as soon as possible, together with all the surface rubbing medicines abundantly prescribed by shortsighted socio-cultural physicians.

The second step consists in an unequivocal recognition that the *sensate form of culture, with its major and minor premises, is not the only great form of culture and is not free from many defects and inadequacies.* Ideational and idealistic forms in their own way are as great as the sensate form.

Third, when one of these forms ages and begins to show signs of its creative exhaustion, as they all do after some period of their domination, *a given culture, in order to continue its creative life, must shift to another basic form of culture—in our case, from the agonizing sensate to the ideational or the idealistic or integral.* Only such a shift can save it from a complete disintegration or mummification. This shift should not be opposed, but should be enthusiastically welcomed as the only escape from a mortal agony.

Fourth, the concerted preparation for the shift implies *the deepest reexamination of the main premises and values of sensate culture, rejection of its superannuated pseudovalues and reenthronement of the real values it has discarded.* The general line of such a reexamination and reevaluation lies in the direction of the integralist conception of truth, reality, and values outlined in . . . [another part of Sorokin's book]. More specifically, it demands an unequivocal recognition that sensory reality and value are but one of the aspects of the infinitely richer true reality and value; that these have a supersensory aspect of which we get a glimpse through our reason and through charismatic grace or intuition in its sublime forms; that this supersensory side is the supreme aspect of the value-reality, and as such it is absolute; that the same is true in regard to the reality and value of man and of the sublimest flowers of his culture. Man is not only an organism but is also a bearer of absolute value. As such, he is sacred and, regardless of sex, age, race, and social status, cannot be used as a mere means for anything or anybody. Likewise, the great values of his culture— science and technology, religion and philosophy, ethics and art—are a reflection, a realization, of the absolute values in the empirical world. As such, they cannot be degraded to mere instrumentalities for purely sensual enjoyment or utility. They are in themselves ends. Since man and his values are sacred, the relationship of man to man should be guided by sublime love, as the categoric imperative. Since truth, goodness, and beauty are absolute values, any further relativization of these, any further degradation to a mere arbitrary convention, becomes out of place. As absolute values they are all one value. Being one, science cannot claim complete freedom from the control of goodness and beauty, and therefore cannot and should not serve any evil purpose. If and when it does so, it misuses its duty and becomes pseudo-science. The same principle applies to art. When it turns into a mere means for sensual pleasure and declares itself free from any moral and cognitive obligations, it degrades itself to mere entertainment, and becomes a pseudo-value. From *the integralist standpoint, the present antagonism between science, religion, philosophy, ethics, and art is unnecessary, not to mention disastrous. In the light of an adequate theory of true reality and value, they all are one and all serve one purpose: the unfolding of the Absolute in the relative empirical world, to the greater nobility of Man and to the greater glory of God. As such they should and can cooperate in the fulfillment of this greatest task.*

Fifth, such a transformation of the mentality of Western culture must naturally be followed by a *corresponding transformation of social relationships and forms of social organization.* The first step here also consists in an unequivocal recognition that all empirical forms of social organization are not absolute but relative values, positive under one set of conditions and negative under another. The same is particularly true of the forms of social-political, economic, and other organizations of superripe sensate culture. Neither Capitalism, nor Socialism, nor Communism, nor Totalitarianism; neither private, nor corporate property; neither mechanical individualism nor mechanistic collectivism is an absolute value. Neither monarchy nor republic,

neither aristocracy nor democracy, neither national state nor international federation can claim to be absolute values. In certain conditions each of these is the best possible form; under other conditions each of these becomes a mere fetish, empty, hollow, even harmful. For instance, such great values as the national state or even private property are at the present time obsolete to a considerable degree. They have outlived the period of their great service to mankind. At the present time they are the sources of social disservice rather than of social well-being. They are the sources of war and revolution, of bloodshed and hatred; even of poverty and misery for the overwhelmingly greater part of mankind—for all except the rulers and the possessors of huge fortunes. Just because man is sacred, no state or its rulers has any right to inflict ruin and misery upon millions for the sake of the aggrandisement of the territory, possession, and power of the state or for that of their own glory. The time of isolated states is past and mankind is already one interacting community. Just because man is sacred, no rich class has a right to enjoy the prodigal life and to hold huge fortunes in its possession while millions of decent, honest, industrious men are jobless, breadless, and devoid of the elementary necessities of life. The interaction and interlocking of the lives and happiness and dignity of all classes of mankind is so close and interdependent at the present time that no such isolation is justifiable or possible any more. This is no recommendation of purely mechanical communistic or totalitarian "socialization and communization" of private property: such mechanical procedures can give only the same disastrous results for society as they have invariably given before. But there must be a change of the whole mentality and attitudes in the direction of the norms prescribed in the Sermon on the Mount. When such a change occurs, to a notable degree the technical ways of remodeling the economic and political structures in this direction become easy. Without this change, no mechanical, politico-economic reconstruction can give the desired results.

And so it is with all the other values that are the means-values for the supreme end-value. Most of these means-values, great at the period of their "spring and summer," are becoming increasingly withered, enfeebled, and sterile. *A transformation of the forms of social relationship, by replacing the present compulsory and contractual relationships with purer and more godly familistic relationships, is the order of the day.* Since coercion expands more and more at the present time, since the contractual relationships have become hollow and decayed, the only way out is a concerted action directed to the introduction of the familistic relationships. Not only are they the noblest of all relationships, but under the circumstances there is no way out of the present triumph of barbarian force but through the realm of familistic relationships. The best methods for making the familistic relationship the foundation of the future society is a purely technical matter not to be discussed here. But for any technical form of social organization to be a way out of the present reign of bloody struggle, it must be a realization of familistic principles. No longer will coercion or the hollow and egotistic contract suffice for the task.

Such, in brief, is the way out of the tragedy. While permitting all the glorious achievements of our sensate culture to live on, such a course will correct the fatal blunders and reestablish the richness, fullness, and manifoldness of true reality

and value. In doing so, it will restore the sanctity of man and his social and cultural mission. Through all that, it eradicates the very root of the malignant growth on our social and cultural life.

Such are the conditions without which the disease cannot be stopped and the tragedy of transition alleviated. There is no doubt that the realization of these means is infinitely more difficult than the application of the superficial measures of economic or political or other "readjustment." *Our remedy demands a complete change of the contemporary mentality, a fundamental transformation of our system of values, and the profoundest modification of our conduct toward other men, cultural values, and the world at large.* All this cannot be achieved without the incessant, strenuous, active efforts on the part of every individual in that direction. Such efforts are incomparably more difficult than a mechanical tampering with economic, political, biological or other conditions. But easy half-measures will always fail, especially in the conditions of a great crisis. The experience of the last few decades shows clearly all the impotency and often even the harmfulness of a host of easy ways out. The more we tampered with economic conditions, the worse they became. The more we outlawed war, the more disastrous it grew. The more social security we tried to establish, the more insecurity we obtained. It is high time to stop deluding ourselves with these easy measures; they have not stopped and cannot stop the process of disintegration. The remedy suggested here is infinitely more difficult, but it is the only one that will prove helpful.

The proposed remedy is based not upon wishful thinking but upon a sound sociological induction: such was the way out during all the comparable crises of the past. It can be reduced to a compact formula: *Crisis — ordeal — catharsis — charisma — resurrection.* The process always consisted in a replacement of the withered root of sensate culture by an ideational or idealistic root, and eventually in a substitution of a full-grown and more spiritual culture for the decadent sensate form. Per contra, in crises of outworn ideational or idealistic cultures the replacement was the reverse: a sensate tree supplanted the ideational or idealistic tree. More explicitly, the problem of overripe sensateness was solved by the emergence of a new religion or by the regeneration of an older religion. The essential reorientation of values, spiritualization of mentality, and ennoblement of conduct were regularly achieved in the form of and through a religious revolution. Virtually all the great world religions either first arose or else experienced their most vital renaissance in periods of profound crisis, as in ancient Egypt at the close of the Old Kingdom and at the end of the Middle Kingdom and of the New Empire, or in Babylonia around the year 1200 B.C. The phenomenon is illustrated more than once by the history of Hindu culture, where each notable crisis was met by a regeneration of Hinduism or by the emergence or revival of Buddhism. The same principle is seen in the history of China, where the crisis of the seventh and sixth centuries B.C. was resolved by the advent of Taoism and Confucianism. Again, in the history of Hebrew culture the crises of the ninth to the fourth century B.C. owe their cure or their partial alleviation to the prophetic religions of Elijah and Elisha; Amos, Hosea, and Isaiah; Ezekiel and Jeremiah; and Ezra and his successors. Finally, to cite an additional instance, the crisis of sensate Greco-Roman culture

was terminated by the growth of Christianity. The respective societies were preserved from dissolution, be it noted, not so much through the "practical and expert" manipulation of economic, political, genetic, or other factors, but mainly through the transmutation of values, the spiritualization of mentality, and the socialization of conduct and ennoblement of social relations effected through the medium of *religion.* Hence the prescribed formula: Crisis — ordeal — catharsis — charisma — resurrection.

Let us trace the course of the revolution in some detail. As has been pointed out in earlier chapters, at the close of the sensate periods of the past the formerly magnificent edifice began to totter. Material pleasures and comforts, utility, security, safety, and freedom progressively declined. War and other forms of strife, brutality, bloodshed, and destruction became endemic. Efforts to patch up the crumbling system invariably miscarried. Under such circumstances people could not fail to perceive eventually the hollowness of sensate culture, the hopelessness of further allegiance to sensate values, and the impossibility of attempting to preserve an orderly way of life on so rotten a foundation. This realization, in turn, led to a defection from the banner of sensate culture and values and to a transfer of allegiance to ideational or idealistic values which appeared to be eternal, indestructible, and independent of anything material and external. Through this fiery ordeal was the catharsis, or purification, of society from its sensate sins and vices finally achieved.

With this catharsis accomplished, there ensued the next phase — that of grace, or charisma. The destructive phase was followed by one that was constructive. The "atomization" of values was replaced by their universalization and "absolutization"; expediency, pleasure, and utility, by duty; licentious freedom, by the sanctity of norms and justice; coercion and egoistic contract, if not by all-embracing, all-bestowing, and all-forgiving love, at least by more familistic and altruistic relationships. Religion, ethics, and law overcame the unbridled sway of force and fraud. God took the place of materialism; spiritual values, that of sensate values. In brief, all the essential sensate values were replaced by less sensate values, either ideational or idealistic.

Purified and ennobled, society proceeded to erect a new house based on the Absolute, God, love, duty, sacrifice, grace, and justice. The poison of decadent sensate culture eliminated, strife and bloodshed diminished, security and safety of life returned, stable order was reestablished, and fresh creative forces were released. Society and individuals were once more at peace with themselves, with their fellow men, with the world, and with God. Thus was ushered in the phase of resurrection, with its long perspective of new creative life.

Such was the invariable course of the great crises of the past. Such is the way out of our own crisis. There is no other possibility.

If human beings were capable of fully profiting by past experience and the lessons of history, the remedy would have been found easily, without the necessity of any fiery ordeal, or even any serious crisis: as soon as the sensate system showed the first signs of decay, the requisite ideational or idealistic reorientation of values, mentality, and conduct would have been willingly undertaken by the society concerned. Unfortunately, "Homo sapiens"[3] seems to be rather purblind so far as the lessons of historical, socio-cul-

tural experience are concerned. He applies and profits by the experience of other persons in matters concerning his physical health. When he is sick, he gives up various pleasures; makes other necessary sacrifices, such as going to bed and taking the prescribed medicine; and behaves in general in a rational manner. He thus frequently avoids much direr consequences, including possibly death itself. In such matters he does not question the existence of causal relationships and causal consequences. Hence he displays neither recklessness nor stupidity, nor does he expect the impossible.

But from the lessons of history concerning life and death, the blossoming and sickness of society, man learns hardly anything. He behaves either as if past history were nonexistent or as if the past presented no situation essentially comparable to that in which his own society finds itself; as if there were no causal relationships and consequences; as if there were no such thing as socio-cultural sickness, and hence no need to sacrifice momentary pleasures and other sensate utilities and values in order to avoid an infinitely great catastrophe. In this field of experience he remains virtually unteachable.

For instance, in the face of the inexhaustible evidence of the ephemeral character of all hastily built empires resting on coercion, men in their purblindness and folly have repeatedly attempted and still attempt to construct eternal empires by precisely such methods. Notwithstanding the perennial failure of efforts effectually to control prices by a mere fiat of the government, such efforts everywhere persist. How many times men have expected to achieve heavenly bliss through a purely mechanical elimination of private property! Yet these experiments are still repeated in spite of their inevitable futility. In the course of human

---

[3] "Man the Reasoner."—Ed.

history several thousand revolutions have been launched with a view to establishing a paradise on earth. And they are still proceeding at full blast, in spite of the fact that practically none of them has ever achieved its purpose. Every page of human history bears witness to wars undertaken in the firm conviction that they would "end war," "abolish despotism," "make the world safe for democracy," overcome injustice, eliminate misery, and the like. And we observe "Homo sapiens" still engrossed in this crazy quest. From this standpoint, the history of human progress is indeed a history of incurable human stupidity!

This unteachableness manifests itself also in the current hope of extricating ourselves from the crisis by means of a variety of facile but shallow artifices, without any fundamental reorientation of values, any thoroughgoing change of mentality and conduct, any persistent personal effort to realize man's divine creative mission on earth instead of acting merely as a "reflex mechanism," or an organism endowed with digestive and sex functions and controlled by its "residues," "drives," and "prepotent reflexes." Hence the crisis itself, and hence the inevitability of a fiery ordeal as the only available means of teaching the otherwise unteachable. *Volentem fata ducunt, nolentem trahunt.*[4] The more unteachable we are, and the less freely and willingly we choose the sole course of salvation open to us, the more inexorable will be the coercion, the more pitiless the ordeal, the more terrible the *dies irae* of the transition. Let us hope that the grace of understanding may be vouchsafed us and that we may choose, before it is too late, the right road—the road that leads not to death but to the further realization of man's unique creative mission on this planet! *Benedictus qui venit in nomine Domini.*[5]

---

[4] "Destiny guides the willing, and drives the unwilling"—Ed.

[5] "Blessed is he who comes in the name of the Lord"—Ed.

Before World War II, WALTER SCHUBART (b. 1897) was an expert on Slavic culture at the University of Riga, Latvia. He married a Russian and converted from the Lutheran to the Eastern Church. Writing in German, Schubart published three books on historical change in Switzerland and one, *Religion und Eros,* in Germany. Although nothing has been heard from Schubart since 1941, he is supposed to be living in the Soviet Union. His books went through several editions, and *Russia and Western Man* has been translated into almost every Western tongue.*

Walter Schubart

The Collapse and Redemption of the West

Promethean man[1] was the first to attempt to rebuild the universe according to human standards, and in doing so he alloted to the human being the same role of Creator and Ruler that he had hitherto assigned to God. Today, this attempt is showing failure all along the line.

In the exact sciences, man has to his surprise been obliged to admit that the more successfully reason analyzes the world into its component parts, the more complicated it becomes, and that behind every problem solved is revealed a greater number of unsolved problems. In the new physics, for instance, the rate of increase of the number of constants is more rapid than that of the dissolution of other quantities, hitherto thought of as constants, into relations connected by law. The number of events that are logically possible increases unceasingly, and today there is no Hercules to stay the Hydra of unsolved problems! The famous physicist de Broglie in his book *Matière et Lumière* (1937) writes: "Whenever, at the cost of great effort, the human mind succeeds in deciphering one page in the Book of Nature, it finds increased difficulty in deciphering the next." The laws of nature in obedience to which,

[1] "I call him Promethean man after those proud Titans who fought against the Gods, the cunning exploiters of the forces of nature, and after the foreseeing one ($\pi\rho o$-$\mu\eta\theta\acute{\eta}\varsigma$), whose ambition was to shape the world according to his own plan," Schubart explained. Spengler called this prototype "Faustian" after Dr. Faustus, the dramatic hero of Marlowe and Goethe. Diez del Corral used both the images of Prometheus and Faust.—Ed.

*From Walter Schubart, *Russia and Western Man,* trans. Amethé von Zeppelin (New York: Frederick Ungar Publishing Co., Inc., 1950). Reprinted by permission. Pp. 285–300.

as it appeared, the world permitted itself to be ruled and exploited, have begun to break down; and it seems that they were mere aids to thought—unnecessary fictions, myths of Promethean man. "What we know as natural laws is merely the sum of the methods that we ourselves have invented in order to appropriate things and subordinate them to our will" (Boutroux, *On the Concept of Natural Law in Contemporary Science and Philosophy*). Thus we have, to our great astonishment, come back to the miracle from which, under the guidance of reason, we had escaped into the realm of calculability. Rationalism refutes itself.

The attempt to rebel against death and disease has also failed. Medical science boasted, not so very long ago, that it had almost succeeded in suppressing infectious disease. Today, we can no longer deny the fact that other maladies like cancer, heart disease, and all kinds of nervous and mental disorders are increasing in the same proportion as the infectious diseases are diminishing. Only the forms of disease change, not their effectiveness. It seems as though the whole organic world were allotted a definite quantum of suffering without which it cannot maintain its balance. It is undoubtedly true that the death rate is falling and that the population of the earth has doubled itself during the last hundred years. But what is the result? Man is stifled and suffocated by his own mass. Nature has revenged herself, inasmuch as man is being crushed by the weight of his own numbers. The balance between the number of the earth's inhabitants and the area of productive land is becoming increasingly disproportionate, with the result that the earth is rapidly becoming too small for its population. The sources of irritation are increasing both in number and in degree of sensitivity; and the effect of this is an increasingly bitter struggle for food-producing land in the atrophy and artificiality of life with its burdensome institutions and organizations without which the vast human masses can no longer be controlled. And at the end of this development, we find one major catastrophe after another—wars and revolutions in which death takes back with brutal force all that science in a wearisome and laborious struggle has managed piece by piece to wrest from him. Death does not permit himself to be bargained with: he takes what belongs to him. That is why the more infrequently wars occur, the more terrible they are when they do occur. No one who attempts to alter, by the methods of calculating reason, the rhythm of death and creation and thereby violates the laws governing the supply and discharge of the life mass, remains unpunished. In the year 1350, the Black Death reduced the population of Europe, in a very short time, from ninety million to sixty-five million. In our century, other forms of catastrophe have given death his due and multiplied his hecatombs. Here again, man has succeeded only in changing the forms of destruction of life and not the facts. Yet the catastrophes of this century are only warning intimations of the ultimate disaster that still lies ahead of us. Man may destroy himself by the very knowledge of nature's processes with which he has hitherto attempted to defeat death! A death dance of macabre humor!

The attempt to establish an earthly kingdom of universal well-being has also failed. No culture hitherto has ever expended so much energy and effort in attempting to achieve material comfort and the satisfaction of mere fleshly desires as the Promethean, which has entirely disregarded the health of the soul.

And no other culture has ever achieved such a degree of human misery! In order to attain his ends, modern man superimposed upon the natural order of things a strange artificial world of substitutes that is known as civilization. At the outset he became inflated by the sensation of immense power; but the further mechanization progressed, the more intense became his uneasiness. Even the Romantic Age, which in its world attitude was the first to attempt to come to terms with the machine, began to show signs of awareness that Europe was taking the wrong path. More and more did this artificial world separate itself from its creator, dispense with him and function solely in obedience to its own laws. In economic life, the firm or enterprise withdrew itself from the human being, became an independent power with its own urge to expansion and forced the individual—even in opposition to his interests—to invest his money "in the business." Whereas in both the Ancient and Gothic worlds there were human beings who worked or did business, in the Promethean world all interest and all business became concentrated on a single aim—the enterprise—in which the human being was absorbed and as a result of which a bleak and hopeless anonymity spread itself over modern life. (It was Promethean man who first proclaimed the rights of the free individual!)

The unaccustomed quality of this new life force engenders in man an oppressive sense of constraint and consequent fear. Man feels himself deflated by the very technical apparatus and organization that he himself has created. In other words, the mechanism has become autonomous and demonic. In the mechanism, the irrational element, which Promethean man thought he had eliminated by means of mechanization, has reappeared. The idea of the autonomy of the machine became an effective one for the first time in Marxist doctrine—in the vague concept of the circumstances of production over which man realized that he no longer had any control. He became aware that he could no longer even cope with them and that he was, like the victim of evil spirits, irretrievably delivered up to them. In the last resort, the whole of Marxism is a single protest against this materialization of mankind, against the victory of the thing over its creator, and against the destruction of the balance between the soul and its environment. Man who desired to conquer nature is today faced with the spectre of anarchy.

Like economics, both technology and national policy today obey their own laws of development, which neither take cognizance of human desires nor indeed consider them at all. The machine has robbed man of his work, organization has taken away his liberty, and both have deprived him of the last vestiges of power. A hundred years ago, man hoped that the machine would serve him like the slaves of old and render him free for a creative life. But although for the accomplishment of many things we require less time than hitherto, we have far less leisure for our own preoccupations. We are no longer masters of the whole process. The machine-made world draws us into its own rhythm, which is no longer commensurate with the rhythm of the organism and which hurls us through life. In America some serious minds have suggested that new inventions, before they are generally released, should be tested as to whether or not they are harmful to the common welfare of humanity. We have become fearful of our own knowledge. We realize now that we cannot look into nature's workshop and steal her patents without suf-

fering for our temerity. Europe is beginning to be aware of something she forgot
in the pride of her inventions, namely,
that the knowledge of nature's processes
multiplies the powers of destruction. And
this is fatal for a culture like the Promethean, which is based upon the awareness of contrast. Gradually, our eyes are
opening to the simple view held by St.
Augustine that science without love is
valueless. In China, the invention of
gunpowder served peaceful ends; in
Europe, it promotes destruction—an
example of the fact that the spiritual
attitude decided the essential nature,
value, and range of importance of a technical achievement. The same methods
cannot be applied to peoples of different
mentalities.

Man as victim of the machine is likewise
victim of organizations. The more indis-
pensible, the more rigid, and the more
widespread the organization, the more
threatening becomes the arbitrariness
with which it is controlled. Even the
concept of justice is suffocated by mass—
by the sheer weight of numbers and
norms. Instead of the hoped-for security
and calculability of existence, modern
man is aware only of demonic forces
encircling him that he can no longer
exorcise.

Even in the year 1812, during the critical weeks pending the outbreak of war,
Napoleon I was confronted with this
phenomenon. He wrote to the Tsar
Alexander I: "One must take precautions;
when events have developed up to a certain point, they are apt to become uncon-
trollable." In 1914, the orders for general
mobilization could no longer "for technical reasons" be reversed; in 1935, Italy's
extensive war preparations forced her
into the war against Abyssinia. It is always
the technical apparatus that forces the
situation. Until the Thirty Years' War,
armies were assembled in order to go to
war; today, wars are embarked upon
because (standing) armies are assembled!
Hence the difficulty that has increased
of late of localizing a conflict. Once the
machinery of war has been set in motion,
it can no longer be controlled at will. It
no longer obeys human behests but the
laws of its own logic. One day therefore—
owing to "technical reasons"—mankind,
whether it desires it or not, will be forced
by this machinery into the final catastrophe.

Not many decades ago we rejoiced at
the conquest of the air. Today, millions
of human beings are trembling again at
the terrifying thought of future bombard-
ments from the air and are spending
enormous quantities of money, energy
and labor in defense measures. And this
at a time when life is organized on a basis
of utility and profit-making! The case
of Icarus, who solved the problem of
flight and was destroyed by it, would
seem about to be repeated.

Technology has entered the phase of
self-destruction. Today, hardly a technical invention exists that is not concerned with war, or is not at least tested
for its usefulness in case of war. Industry
is now chiefly concerned with the production either of means of destruction or
of defense measures against destruction.
The expenditure on armaments is colossal, and the young men of today are sac-
rificing an increasing part of their scientific training to comply with military
requirements. Many national enterprises
are maintained only because they are
essential to war production. The world
armed itself in order to get rid of the
problem of unemployment; and it must
continue to arm in order to continue to
employ labor! In this way, the economic
system is maintained in a healthy condition! One must not, however, mistake

the hectic flush of a consumptive for the healthy color of a chubby-faced youth!

Promethean Europe is now faced with a choice between rearmament, which will inevitably lead to war, and disarmament, with the resulting dismissal from employment, which will lead to Bolshevism. In other words: man has only a choice between the forms of his downfall. He has actually already made his decision in favor of armaments and war and is trying to save his life by preparing for his final destruction. He thereby postpones his ultimate destiny—but it will be all the more terrible when it comes upon him. Europe is like the debtor who, in order to extract himself from the embarrassment of the moment borrows money from the usurer at a rate of interest that will certainly ruin him.

The final efforts of Western culture are now concentrated solely on the aim to destroy the vast technical apparatus by means of which man has succeeded in withdrawing himself, in equal measure, from both heaven and earth. Everything is designed to make the universal wars of the future as thorough, exhausting and destructive as possible, to drag into them the maximum number of human beings, including women and children, and to invest in them the greatest possible number of material and spiritual goods. (When military science "calls up" for a total war, it becomes the direct instrument of the aims of Providence.) The last and dominating science in Europe within the framework of technological science, has become the technique of destruction. The power of technological science has arisen against mankind; the creature is destroying the creator! A Golem tragedy on a world-historical scale!

Western culture is yearning for self-destruction; although everything mortal is transitory, the form of its downfall is characteristic of it alone. Western culture will not, like that of the Incas or Aztecs, be overpowered by foreign invaders. Nor will it succumb to old age like the Roman civilization. It will die by its own hand in the heyday of its strength. This suicide of an entire culture is unique in history, and Goethe was aware of it when he wrote: "I see the time coming when God will have no further pleasure in mankind and will be forced to smash everything in order to start creating anew."

Promethean culture is being destroyed by a unique species that I have designated as "object-minded mankind," an expression that unites in itself the two concepts of extraversion and materialism. When man—the most exhausted vitally of all living beings, nature's sick creature —began to feel that he could no longer continue to develop his organs, he turned to his brain and invented tools with which to carry on his existence. That was the birthday of technology, which secured for the human being his survival in the struggle with the animal world and with climatic conditions. Only in a later stage of development, when he began to feel an inward sense of security, did man become thoughtful and meditative concerning the nature and meaning of existence. That was the birthday of spiritual and intellectual culture. At that moment of history, a higher order of existence made itself known to man, an existence essentially different from the material world. It was the fatal mistake of Promethean man that he refused all further knowledge of this order of existence and continued on the path that began with the invention of tools and that failed to guide him out of the material world. Western culture withdrew itself from God and the spiritual life into the inorganic world below and finally became active on a level below that of the spiritual realm. (That which it called mind, or spirit, was merely practical intelligence, or the talent for inventing tools—of the highest perfection, no doubt!) This lower realm of nature and the laws governing it are responsible for the downfall of Promethean mankind. As soon as man leads a purely material existence and suppresses the eternal in himself, he loses all detachment from the world of substance in which he has become involved; he becomes a piece of matter in a material world—mere mass which is overcome by larger masses. He parts with the one thing that distinguishes him from all other beings—the divine spirit and the possibility of freedom. When he regarded the world as a mechanism he did not, at first, feel that he was part of this machine, whirring along with it, but rather looked upon himself as the mechanic servicing the machine. The new world outlook inspired in him a sensation of complete power; he regarded the world as God regards the human being—as a creature. But it is not possible to remain outside the material world as its master if one denies the essential antithesis between man and machine, between soul and thing. Promethean man sought to attain freedom through his power over matter. But in the end it was matter that acquired power over the human being who had enslaved himself. The question here is one of a false concept of freedom.

Freedom is not power, but renunciation—it is liberation from the power of things. (Thucydides relates that the Lydians became slaves because they were incapable of saying "no.") Power in itself enslaves: the master depends upon the slave. This was felt by Sulla, Diocletian, Charles V, and the Tsars Ivan IV and Alexander I, to mention only a few names. He alone is free who withdraws

himself from the world of substance and is at home with the soul in the divine realm of the spirit. In order to maintain the freedom of His spirit, Jesus renounced His power over an earthly kingdom. That is the meaning of the second temptation in the wilderness (Luke IV, 5–8).

With the transition from the Gothic to the Promethean Age, from the harmonious to the heroic culture, man repeated the sins recorded in the Bible. He sacrificed the freedom of Paradise in order to become like God. And now, at the end, he finds himself once more the slave of labor. The curse of original sin weighs upon modern Western civilization and affects all who come into contact with it, whether they be Russians, North American Indians, South Sea Islanders, Negroes, or Eskimos. Finally, the deadly effect becomes directed against Western man himself. The germ of death was already present in the early stages of Promethean culture, in the primitive experience of Promethean man, and in his view of the ego and the world as antithesis. It was this attitude of antithesis that cast Europe into the tragedy of a war of self-annihilation—in the seventeenth, nineteenth and twentieth centuries. There is nothing parallel to this in any other culture, and it is the same attitude that will bring about the universal war of the future in which Western civilization will extinguish itself.

Promethean man has begun to be aware of his coming downfall. He is trying to escape from reflection and from solitude. He is endeavoring to escape through narcotics into pleasure, work, or into the crowd. Only not to be free—only not to feel any responsibility! Rather obedience and slavery! He is not only a slave, but he desires to be one! He is grateful to Caesar for depriving him, with his freedom, of the torture of self-determination.

He embraces the whip that flays him. That is the essential nature of contemporary collectivism, which is a compulsory association of slaves and has nothing in common with true community, which is always a free community of brothers.

An apocalyptic atmosphere hangs over the whole earth today. We are all haunted by the consciousness of an approaching doom from which we are unable to save ourselves. The security of life that modern man dreamed of, and that earthly order of existence that was regarded as the permanent possession of mankind, are gone. Political history is once more being enacted in the crudest forms that we erroneously regarded as characteristic of times long past and outlived. Instead of the dynastic, constitutional, and economic motives with which we had become familiar, racial hatred has now, as in primitive times, become a prime consideration in power politics. Flogging has been reintroduced; innocent women and children are being maltreated for motives of revenge against their husbands and fathers. And all this in a culture of personalities which had proclaimed that each individual is responsible only for himself! Wars are once more started without any declaration of war—as in the days of invasion by the Huns and Tartars—and are directed, as in barbaric times, against women, children and old people. Religion has once more taken on the aspect of martyrdom, and things, in all their uncertainty and problematic nature, are being revealed to their foundations.

What did we know of death? We knew him only in frock coat and top hat, as well mannered and civilized as ourselves! When we sat in school and read in the Latin classics of banishment, expulsion and exile, of spies and confiscation, had we a clear picture of the meaning of these words? When we read in the Bible of God-fearing men who were killed for loyalty to their religious beliefs, had we any idea of what this meant? Today, all these terrible aspects of history have come alive again, long after they had become so far removed from us that we could almost see them disappearing into the mists of legend! Now, everything is just as problematical as it was at the beginning of culture, and life has once more reverted to its original state of unrest. Even the purely animal horror of death and the fear for freedom, home and property, which had been forgotten, have come into their own again. At the same time, ever since the nineteenth century, we have carried with us the fading phantom of a just and stable world in comparison with which the recurring chaos, in view of this development, reveals itself in its full corruption. How ridiculous it seems to talk about the "lightening of the political horizon" when somewhere in Europe two ministers of different states exchange a few polite formalities! The approaching collapse of Western culture is unavoidable, and we may even ask ourselves whether it would be desirable to avoid it. Ought we not to beg, and even to pray, for the judgment of God and for the punishment of humanity? For there can be no resurrection of mankind except from the depths of torment. Doctrine is of very little use, example aids a little more, but distress and suffering are of the greatest help. Just as enormous quantities of concentrated energy are necessary to split the nucleus of the atom, so great events are required in order to sever the links binding religious feeling to those transitory values manifested in myths and pseudo-religions. But these religious forces must be liberated or no new creation can become possible.

The farseeing members of the human race are suffering today from the fact that their warning voices do not reach those who wield the power that molds history. The voice of wisdom is silenced by hopelessly blinded authorities. Thus— as so often before—it is once more the tragic fate of prophets to see the misfortune approaching without being able to prevent it, and it is the equally tragic destiny of the actors in the drama that they are unable to see the misfortunes they themselves are causing. Impotent seers—unsuspecting rulers! But there is a deeper meaning in all this. If the warning voices were not to fall on deaf ears, the ultimate collapse would not be so certain. But it is certain—and is probably better so. We, for our part, welcome everything that will ensure the downfall of Promethean culture. Of course, we, who desire this downfall, must also desire to be in the forefront of its penitents and victims. It would be mean and unworthy of us to put into a safe harbor from which, like Carovius in Jacob Wassermann's *Gänsemännchen,*[2] we might savor the reports of other misfortunes as a special delicacy!

The twentieth century is a truly tragic century. The last century was saved from the knowledge of approaching downfall by illusion of progress and by an increase in material well-being. The next century will have survived the catastrophe and will look back upon our path of error with a certain feeling of relief. But we ourselves are rushing towards the abyss and are unable to stop ourselves. We know, or are beginning to be aware of the fact, that ours is the path of death; but we no longer have any chance of turning from it. We are driven onwards by the unmerciful momentum of the centuries and are being hurled into the depths.

The ultimate settlement between the East and the West has thus far manifested itself in four stages. We have seen in Russia the Eastern spirit repulsing the Western mentality (stage I). In Europe, we saw the first signs of a fundamental change in outlook (stage II), and, at the same time, Promethean civilization preparing its own downfall (stage III). Finally, as the result of their struggle against the West, we see the Russians themselves changing. While the Occident is gradually acquiring a more spiritual, Eastern outlook, the Russians are manifesting a number of new qualities of a more Western character. The contact with Western culture has forced the Russian to adapt himself to its predominant characteristics and even, at times, to adopt them in order to overcome their more harmful aspects. No battle has ever been fought from which the victor has emerged as he was at the outset: he is always, in some measure, changed by his vanquished enemy. Dying epochs and declining cultures continue to live as a result of having forced their successors to overcome them. Here, as always, death and birth are interwoven with one another and, in the end, the stirrings of new life can always be felt. As in the lowest forms of life, so in the apocalyptic stage of an epoch, death and procreation are united in conception and new life. Not only the agony, but also the ecstasy of death is a sign of the pregnance that heralds a new being coming into existence. In the twentieth century, the interdependence of love and death is manifested in the fate of a whole generation. And therefore Europe has no reason to feel that she is the victim of history.

In Russia, a type of humanity is developing which is neither that of the period prior to 1917 nor prior to 1689, but a quite new species with an Eastern soul that has been influenced by Western culture as by a hardening process. This new type, while truly Russian, is yet heir

---

[2] Title of a German novel published in 1915—Ed.

to the eternal values of the West. A man of this type is inspired by his inborn Slav nature, but not less so by the conflicts and contradictions of European civilization. And it is only he who, as a new type of humanity, will be capable of uttering the word of reconciliation in the settlement of the problem of the East and West. For although the Russian of today is not as yet the Man of the Millennium, yet it is he—and only he—who will succeed in evolving him; the Russian will purify himself until he has attained the height of development necessary to produce him. Even sworn enemies of Bolshevism, like Solonevitch, speak of the "strong generation" growing up in the Soviet Republic—a generation no longer characterized by the repellent, proverbial Russian indolence, that degenerated form of primitive trust.

The new generation is full of energy and fired with enthusiasm for all efforts made in the direction of reconstruction. The Stakhanov movement, the *Udarniki* and the *Olitshniki* (*élite* workers) are all manifesting a growing interest in their work and developing a sense of duty in every branch of activity, instead of their previous indifference. A consciousness of the dignity of labor has superseded the servile attitude of former times, as well as all nihilistic tendencies. Possibly, the old Oblomov has not as yet become completely extinct—he probably still lives on in the Russian mania for speechifying, or in Russian wish-dreams: "How would it be if . . ."; or "Come again in three months or so . . . and then. . . ."! Administration is probably still undeveloped, and the average worker may not as yet possess a proper sense of responsibility and may even rob his own state. But one thing is quite certain and that is that the Russian is well on the way to transforming his life, which had be-

come nihilistic in character, into something positive. This has been achieved by the Bolshevist Revolution, which gave the Russians a sense of reality, accustomed them to this attitude and gained their co-operation for immediate aims. It forced them to take life seriously. If in earlier days the Russian laughed and mocked at the idea of this "little poor world," he is now passing through a phase belonging to the other extreme: he is harnessed in the service of the earth and dedicated to the conquest of its material wealth. Efficiency, punctuality and precision are now the most highly prized qualities in Russia. This period of disciplinary effort on the behalf of the Here and the Now was necessary in order that the Russians might become aware of their nihilistic despair, which was destructive of everything. And it is for this reason that those characteristics which made them—not without good reason—contemptible, and even insupportable, in the eyes of Europe, are being driven out of them with scorpions!

What Madame de Stäel said of nations is equally true of epochs and of cultures of those epochs, namely, that they possess the virtues of their failings and the failings of their virtues. The spiritual Russian needs practical qualities; the practical European is in the need of a new humanity. He who strives only after inner perfection, fails in the performance of daily tasks; through too much virtue he is rendered useless for everyday life. One must reconcile the Russian with the world in order that he may no longer desire its end. On the other hand, one must seek to withdraw the European from the world in order that he may not expend himself wholly on the details of temporal existence. The Russian must become more efficient, the European more virtuous. The Russian must learn to concentrate his "universal" feeling, the Westerner to expand his "point" attitude. The one must learn to recognize and honor the earth, the other must learn to look heavenwards.

Efficiency without virtue, achievement without humanity—both represent a great danger. In the hands of a human being without love unlimited power must inevitably lead to destruction. And all his intellectual achievements, if they be not curbed by moral principles, are liable to become directed towards violence and death. Promethean culture, too efficient to be able to withstand the effects of a lack of humanity, is being destroyed by the disproportion between virtue and efficiency.

The question whether a settlement between the East and the West—or a synthesis of the two—is possible, may be extended to the more general question whether virtue and efficiency can be combined. The problem is to discover the spiritual attitude in which we can be efficient without violating the tenets of moral behavior, Here is the problem for a future ethic. The Gothic Age is proof enough that it is a soluble one. The reconciliation of virtue and efficiency is founded upon the restitution of the harmonious attitude toward life that prevailed during the Gothic era.

The settlement between the East and the West does not demand any loss of individuality on either side. Neither does it mean that Europe must become a part of Russia, or that Russia should sell herself to the West. It merely means that two spiritual potencies should strive to reach one another—two original forms of spiritual being that, in order to be creative, must come into contact with one another. It is like man and woman, who, if they do not come together, cannot generate new life.

Western man has achieved things of irreplaceable value in the external order of life—in economics, in all technical matters, in political economy, in social structure and organization. He has achieved things that will remain the permanent possession of humanity. But while concentrating on the external world, Western man has sacrificed his soul; hence, a large proportion of his technical achievements has lost its value. While the technical development in travel and communications between the different countries of the world has reduced distances to a minimum and has made possible the rapid exchange of spiritual and material goods, political and economic opinion in the Promethean culture has separated them more violently than ever. Measures such as the refusal of permits of exit and entry, currency restrictions, customs regulations, and so on, have crippled all facilities of travel and communication to such an extent that a journey from Berlin to Rome, or from Paris to Moscow, although theoretically it can be accomplished in a few hours, requires in fact many weeks of preparation at the end of which it may still be impossible to undertake! We see here quite plainly that technical development has capitulated to the "point" attitude and can achieve nothing without the all-embracing soul. Only the soul can overcome the forces of division and disruption.

The Russian is faced with quite the opposite type of danger. Close as he is to external things, he is liable to lose contact with temporal existence. The effect of this is that he either withdraws himself altogether from temporal life, like the Russian monk, or he proceeds to attack it with violence and is hurled into nihilism like the Russian revolutionary. These are the two great dangers that beset all human beings of the end cultures. And against these, the rational character of Promethean man, who is by nature subservient to compulsory forms, is the most effective protection.

Russia—not the present but the future—is the refreshing wine capable of renewing the exhausted life of modern humanity; Europe is the durable vessel in which to preserve the wine. Without the solid form to keep it together the wine would be spilled over the country; without the wine that fills it the precious cup remains an empty and cold showpiece alienated from its purpose. Only when wine and cup meet can mankind most fully enjoy them.

Modern Europe is form without life; Russia is life without form. In the first instance, the soul has escaped from the form, or mold, and has left an empty dwelling behind. In the second, life has burst all the bonds, but has achieved no new form or mold. We maintain, therefore, that the renewal of humanity, which is conditioned by a settlement between the East and the West, depends chiefly on Russia—on life rather than on form. Not the European, but the Russian, possesses the fundamental attitude through which man will eventually discover the true purpose of his existence. The Russian mind is directed towards the Absolute—he has "universal" feeling and a Messianic soul. Hence, we repeat that in all essential questions of life, the European must accept the Russian as a model—and not the other way round. If he desires to find his way back to eternal values, the European must acknowledge the world outlook of the Russian. It was this that Dostoievsky meant when he demanded that every single one of earth's inhabitants should first of all be a Russian!

Let us remind ourselves once more that the Englishman desires the world as a factory, the Frenchman as a salon, the German as an army barracks, the Russian as a church. The Englishman seeks gain, the Frenchman fame, the German power, and the Russian sacrifice. The Englishman desires to exploit his neighbor, the Frenchman to impress him, the German to command him—only the Russian desires nothing from him. The Russian has no desire to use his fellow men as the means to an end. And this is the core of the idea of brotherhood and brotherliness. This is also the gospel of the future and the great moral counterforce to be pitted against the Latin ideas of the "man of Power" and the "power state." The Russian as a universal human being is the representative of a new solidarity; and he alone can liberate mankind from the individualism of the superman and the collectivism of mass humanity. Against the autonomous personality of the Renaissance he sets the soul that is united with the Whole; and against the compulsory association of human beings he sets the free community of souls that are united with the Whole. He thus creates both a new concept, and a new ideal of personality and freedom.

Our age has often been compared with that of the decline of ancient Rome and rightly so. But in making this comparison, one should not only think of the shadows—there are other similarities that are full of light. During the period of the decline and downfall of the Roman Empire, the forces of East and West were hurled against one another with a violence that proved fatal. But the teachings of Egypt and Greece nevertheless reached the Parthians and the Chinese. The wisdom of Ancient India crossed the Nile in a westerly direction, and the cults of Isis and Mithra, as well as the Gospel of the Nazarene, found their way to the capital of the Roman Empire—to the seat of decadence. It was an epoch of contradictions, of currents and cross-currents, of rise and fall, of death and decay —but also one of Messianic promise. The twentieth century is a kindred epoch. A new Apocalypse is approaching with a Last Judgment—and a Resurrection!

Promethean man already bears upon his brow the sign of Death. Now let the Man of the Millennium be born!

From 1931 to 1938 the anthropologist ALFRED L.
KROEBER worked on his *Configurations of Culture
Growth* (1944), a sociological philosophy of history
later to be amplified by *Style and Civilizations* (1957).
These final pages from a paper Kroeber delivered
in 1958 reflect the wide range of his inquiries as well
as his cautious conclusions.*

Alfred L. Kroeber

Flow and Reconstitution
within Civilizations

The characteristic forms of culture which are non-repetitive, plastic, and creative, are its styles. Styles are characterized first by internal consistency; second by the property of growth; and third, by a quality of irreversibility: they can develop but they cannot "disdevelop" or turn back. All three of these qualities—consistency, growth, and irreversibility—are characteristic also of organisms; though this similarity is only analogous, since organisms are animals or plants functioning through physiology and heredity, whereas styles are social products of the one species of organism, man.

Civilizations contain more or less repetitive elements in which the qualities of style are present only feebly or transiently; but they not only do also contain styles, but on their creative dynamic side they consist characteristically of styles. They may be described accordingly as a collocation or association of styles; and in proportion as this association is integrated, we can usefully regard a civilization as a sort of superstyle, or master style, possessing some degree of over-all design and being set, faced, or sloped in a specific and more or less unique direction.

A civilization would presumably partake of the qualities of the styles of which it is composed. Besides the consistency or coherence which we have just mentioned, civilizations should then show also the property of growth; and this property they are indeed generally credited with. Finally, civilizations might

*From A. L. Kroeber, *An Anthropologist Looks at History* (Berkeley and Los Angeles: University of California Press, 1963), pp. 56–59. Reprinted by permission of The Regents of the University of California.

114

share with styles the property of irreversibility; and this is the problem we have set ourselves to inquire into.

There are well-defined civilizations, such as the ancient Egyptian, which have dissolved away and sooner or later have been replaced by others. As integrated entities, they have long been what we popularly call them: dead. We may describe their death as due to the exhaustion of the potentialities in the superstyle which is the most significant part of a civilization. This would be construed as analogous to the ultimate exhaustion, within any particular creative style, of the potentialities to which it is committed in virtue of being a style. With its creativity exhausted, a civilization is either taken over and absorbed and thus replaced by another; or its patterns as well as its styles dilapidate, crumble, and collapse into confusion. Such periods in which processes of disorganization prevail over constructive organization are like the interregnum called the Dark Ages which followed Graeco-Roman civilization and preceded our own Western civilization.

We have reviewed and on the whole confirmed the similarity alleged between the post-culmination condition of Graeco-Roman civilization of 200 B.C. to A.D. 200 and the contemporary condition of our own, with its growing sense of crisis, and in some quarters fear of doom. In ancient times this condition was followed from A.D. 200 to 500 by increasing collapse of cultural patterns and organization, further followed, from 500 to about 900, by the Dark Age of amorphous chaos of civilization in Western Europe. Another collapse and Dark Age may therefore seem to loom ahead for us.

However, an alternative parallel or analogue is furnished by the period of Reconstitution which Western civilization underwent from about 1300 to 1550, after the style patterns of its High Mediaeval Phase had been exhausted, and from which its Modern Phase emerged with reorientation and a broadened set of patterns. This period of Reconstitution — of which the Renaissance was one part — was also a time of strain, conflict, crisis, uncertainties, and loosening of patterns. However, population, wealth, curiosity, knowledge, enterprise, and invention continued to grow during the period. These advances were concurrent with the dissolution of the exhaused Mediaeval style patterns; with the result that new sets of patterns were being evolved as the worn-out ones were being abandoned; and thus a second phase of Western civilization was successfully launched. The contrast with the Graeco-Roman course of events is that there the exhaustion and breakdown of style patterns was accompanied not by expansion but by contraction of population, wealth, curiosity, knowledge, enterprise, and invention. Thus the critical period became one of Collapse instead of Reconstitution.

When now we match the present condition of our civilization comparatively against these two analogues, it seems fairly clear that the correspondence is greater with the European stage of Reconstitution than with the Graeco-Roman stage of Dissolution. This is because now, as in 1300–1550, population, wealth, curiosity, knowledge, enterprise, and invention are definitely still in an expanding phase. It seems somewhat likely, accordingly, that we are now in the throes of a second stage of Reconstitution of our civilization. In that case, period Western Civilization II would already be mainly past, whether we so recognize it or not, and period Western Civilization III lies ahead of us whenever we shall have finished reorganizing our cultural style patterns with a resultant new over-all set or direction.

Of course all historical prediction, or even contemporary diagnosis, must remain approximate and tentative, since correspondences are never wholly parallel in history, and since it is of the nature of history to show analogies while disguising any homologies it may contain. Still, the preponderance of correspondence does seem to be as set forth, so that we may reasonably incline toward the inference that it is the symptoms of a stage of major reconstitution that are alarming us.

ERIC HOFFER (b. 1902) grew up in New York City; he
was "practically blind up to the age of fifteen," and
"had no schooling." When he recovered his eyesight,
Hoffer "read indiscriminately everything within reach
—English and German." Orphaned early, Hoffer went
west and spent most of his life as migratory worker,
gold-miner, and finally longshoreman in San Francisco,
reading and writing in his spare time. Besides *The
Temper of Our Time* (1967), a collection of essays
which appeared in various magazines, Hoffer has
published *The True Believer* (1951), *The Passionate
State of Mind and Other Aphorisms* (1955), and *The
Ordeal of Change* (1963). Recently Hoffer appeared
on national television and before congressional
committees as a commentator on contemporary mass
movements and social unrest.*

Eric Hoffer

The Mystery of the Occident

The decline of the Occident has been proclaimed on housetops for over half a century. Knowledgeable people are still telling us that Europe is finished, America rotten to the core, and that the future is in Russia, China, India, Africa, and even in Latin America. We are urged to learn the meaning of life from these bearers of the future. Yet it is becoming evident that if there is going to be anywhere a genuine growth of individual freedom and human dignity it will be from cuttings taken from the Occident. Even the Communist parties of the Occident are discovering that their historical role is not to change the Occident's way of life but to put a brake on the dehumanizing juggernaut of the Communist apparatus in Russia and China.

The fact is that the awakening of Asia and Africa has turned the Occident into a mystery. When we see to what ugly stratagems the new countries have to resort in order to make their people do the things which we consider natural and matter-of-fact we begin to realize how unprecedented the Occident is with its spontaneous enterprise and orderliness, and its elementary decencies. The mystery of our time is not the enigmatic Orient but the fantastic Occident.

The Occident is at present without fervent faith and hope. There is no overwhelming undertaking in sight that might set minds and hearts on fire. There is no singular happiness and no excessive suffering. We have already discounted every possible invention, and reduced momentous tasks to sheer routine. Though we are aware of deadly dangers ahead of us, our fears have not affected our rhythm of life. The Occident continues to function well at room temperature.

Now, there are those who maintain that lack of a strong faith must in the long run prove fatal to a society, and that the most decisive changes in history are those which involve a weakening or intensification of belief. Whether this be true or not it should be clear that a weakening of faith can be due as much to a gain in power, skill, and experience as to a loss of vigor and drive. Where there is the necessary skill and equipment to move mountains there is no need for the faith that moves mountains. Intensification of belief is not necessarily a symptom of vigor, nor does a fading of belief spell decline. The strong, unless they are infected with a pathological fear, cannot generate and sustain a strong faith. Nowhere in the Occident is there at present a faith comparable to that which is being generated in the meek, backward masses of Russia and China. The Occident has skill, efficiency, orderliness, and a phenomenal readiness to work. It would be suicidal for the Occident to rely on a concocted new faith in a contest with totalitarian countries. We can prevail only by doing more and better what we know how to do well. Those in the Occident who wring their hands and pray for a new faith are sowing the wind.

Free men are aware of the imperfection inherent in human affairs, and they are willing to fight and die for that which is not perfect. They know that basic human problems can have no final solutions, that our freedom, justice, equality, etc. are far from absolute, and that the good life is compounded of half measures, compromises, lesser evils, and gropings toward the perfect. The rejection of approximations and the insistence on absolutes are the manifestation of a nihilism that loathes freedom, tolerance, and equity.

H. STUART HUGHES (b. 1916), professor of Modern
European History at Harvard University, studied at
Heidelberg, Munich, and Paris before receiving his
Ph.D. from Harvard in 1940. He saw wartime service
as research officer in Italy and Germany. In 1946 he
became chief of the Division of Research for Europe
in the Department of State in Washington, and in
1948 he was appointed Associate Director of the Russian
Research Center at Harvard. Out of this close
acquaintance with Europe grew his critical estimate of
the sources, influence, and significance of Spenglerism,
first published in 1952. Hughes' other works include
An Essay for Our Time (1950), *The United States and
Italy* (1953), *Consciousness and Society* (1958),
Contemporary Europe: A History (1961), and *An
Approach to Peace* (1962).*

H. Stuart Hughes

Spengler and His Successors

Spengler's successors as cyclical theorists have based their work on philosophical presuppositions radically different from his. All of them regard their intellectual constructions as "scientific" —that is, having some claim to objective validity. In their selection and evaluation of data, they have conscientiously tried to apply the recognized canons of scientific method, and they are convinced that their conclusions represent a fair approximation of the "truth." Nor do they adopt the more pragmatic, experimentalist definition of science—the notion of truth as an effective guide to action based on an average of long experience—to which so many contemporary historians and sociologists adhere. Both Sorokin and Kroeber apparently regard their conclusions as having something more than a merely experimental validity. In this sense, they are both positivists. And the same is basically true of Toynbee—although in his case the question is complicated by his apparent hesitation between writing "scientific" history and writing a history of salvation.

In contrast to these three, the *Decline* makes no claim to scientific validity. For Spengler, the essence of history remains a mystery. The best the historian can hope for is through the construction of inspired metaphors to catch a reflection of the ultimate truth that will always elude him. In history, Spengler affirms, we do not ask, as in natural science, whether a theory is true or false: we ask simply whether it is "profound" or "super-ficial." The distinction is approximately the same as the contrast we have already observed between the "systematic" and "physiognomic" approaches. In Speng-lerian terms, all of his successors may be described as systematic writers; he alone follows the physiognomic method.

Yet the distinction is not quite so clear-cut as that. It holds only when Spengler is at his most consistent—when he is being true to the sceptical implications of his own thought. At other times, the positivist remainder in his intellectual heritage leads him to make assertions of a totally opposite character. To be con-sistent with his own philosophic ap-proach, even Spengler's determinism should be phrased in subjective terms: it should not go beyond the statement that to a historian writing in Germany in the second decade of the twentieth century, it appeared that certain past developments could have happened in no other fashion, and that a certain succession of future events was inescap-able. But from time to time Spengler implies much more than that: he leaves his readers with the impression that things actually *happened* as he said they happened, and that the future *must* be as he said it would be. When Spengler writes in this fashion, he is even more positivist than his positivist competitors, since he is more dogmatic.

But at other times, Spengler quite clearly limits the range of his own omni-science. He recognizes that the validity of his theoretical scheme cannot tran-scend the historical circumstances of its composition. "Every living perception," he writes, "including the one I have pro-posed, belongs to one single time." And in asserting the "truth" of what he has discovered, he claims no more than that it is *"true for me,* and as I believe, true

for the leading minds of the coming time; not true in itself as dissociated from the conditions imposed by blood and by history, for that is impossible." He will not quite say that it is all simply his own personal idea. But he limits himself to the assertion that his theories peculiarly fit the intellectual temper of the present time and that future thinkers will more and more be led to adopt them. And this latter claim has found some substantia-tion in the surprising uniformity with which subsequent cyclical theorists have developed ideas roughly paralleling those of the *Decline.* When he writes in this fashion, Spengler is actually more modest than his successors, however much the hesitancy and reasonableness of their literary tone may contrast favor-ably with his. At his most consistent, Spengler is more sceptical than they are, and more sophisticated in his use of his-torical terminology. His relativist method penetrates more radically and responds more closely to the contemporary de-mand for critical detachment. This is the guise in which Spengler can best pre-sent his own case for continued intel-lectual currency.

Considered in this light, Spengler's view of the cyclical historian's role ap-pears better thought-out than that of his successors. It would be difficult for any critically-minded historian—whether positivist, idealist, or simple sceptic—to accept the very notion of a scientific cyclical theory. Or at least he could ac-cept it only if he were to define the word "scientific" in contemporary pragmatic terms. Yet no one to date appears to have ventured to construct a cyclical theory on these premises. This reluc-tance is more than accidental: tempera-mentally and by the very nature of his method, a pragmatist would find him-self at a loss to elaborate an all-inclusive theory of history. His whole emphasis on plural explanations and on attacking each problem on its own merits, would preclude the attempt. Almost inevitably, then, cyclical history falls either into the positivist or into the relativist-mystical category—or into personal combinations of the two. These two attitudes alone appear to offer the requisite dosage of temerity or imaginative scepticism. The middle position that to most contemporary social scientists might seem the most sensible, simply fails to figure in the problem.

Hence it is not going too far to state that the cyclical theories devised up to the present time are all highly personal constructions, based on uncertain and ill-defined criteria of analysis, and having their origin in intuition. They can be called scientific under none of the usual definitions of that term. As Kroeber, alone of Spengler's successors, has recognized, a general theory of history can attain the required degree of systematic precision only on narrow and detailed questions, where some sort of quantitative measurement is possible. Yet even here the selection of evidence injects a huge element of personal arbitrariness and fallibility. If this is so, then obviously the large and really interesting questions fall entirely outside the sphere of the scientific method. On them, the individual historian's creative imagination holds virtually unlimited sway.

Ultimately, then, we may conclude that all cyclical theorists, whether or not they lay claim to scientific validity, play the role of intuitive seers. They are all doing what Spengler alone quite frankly says he is doing. If we decide to adopt this attitude toward them, then we shall judge them far differently from the way in which they have generally been judged up to now. We shall worry far less about the mistakes, the irritating dogmatism, of a writer like Spengler than we should do if we imagined that he and his kind were about to deliver themselves of some sort of final truth. We shall discount his errors and try to appreciate the positive suggestions he can offer. In fact, once we have adopted such an attitude of radical scepticism, we may learn to esteem and relish even the dogmatism of Spengler's utterance. Since we shall not take what he says too literally, we may find that the very intemperance of his statements enhances their imaginative impact.

From this standpoint, we may take our choice of the cyclical constructions on frankly non-scientific grounds. We may judge them first as literature, as imaginative creations, second as prophecies of varying degrees of discernment. On both these grounds, Spengler comes off rather well.

As literature, the *Decline* is without equal in the field of cyclical writing. Spengler's pictorial, figurative language, his talent for finding the images and personalities that set off in high relief an entire epoch of the past—these give to his work a character of excitement, of tension, and of evocative melancholy. He is a master of the telling epithet, of contrasts epitomized in a single abstract noun, of the alternation of involved, architectural sentences with the short hammer blows of unqualified assertion. In its final form the *Decline* becomes the elaborate reconstruction of a vision, a series of "perspectives"—as Spengler himself puts it—shot boldly into the past and future. Even for those who do not choose to follow them to their ultimate conclusions, these perspectives may illuminate the understanding and offer guidance for fresh investigation. The "Magian" culture may never have existed

—but we may use the concept to deepen our imaginative comprehension of a variety of seemingly unrelated manifestations in the art and religion of the Mediterranean world. True or false, such creations as these have permanently enriched our understanding of our past and of our future.

It is not true, as Spengler once boasted, that he had been proved mistaken "on no essential point." Two at least of his predictions have quite obviously failed to materialize. In Western Europe, parliamentary institutions—despite signs of advanced anemia—have to date continued to function. And the major armies of the world have not reduced themselves to small, supranational, strictly personal followings; they are still combinations of mass and professional forces, finding their indispensable support in the patriotic sentiments and industrial productivity of national populations. Here and there, however, bands of expatriated mercenaries, inspired with the desperation of permanent exile from their own country, such as General Anders' Poles of the Second World War and Chiang Kai-shek's Chinese of today, have offered a preliminary view of what may prove to be the new model. These things may be still in the future. But in more general terms we may conclude that Spengler's failure to establish a number of vital links in the sequence of future events reflects the inadequacy of his personal preconceptions. His faulty economics, his "metaphysical" and unrealistic definition of social classes, drastically limit his comprehension of twentieth-century political movements. As a result, his notion of Caesarism remains too much a matter of mere personal leadership to embrace in its entirety the contemporary phenomenon of totalitarianism.

Yet, as with the overwhelming majority of the predictions in the *Decline,* the basic idea is there even when the formulation is faulty. More poignantly than any of his successors, Spengler has sensed the unprecedented character of our time —the resurgence of those primitive values that so sharply divide the twentieth century from the centuries that went before it. This feeling for essentials extends even to his less fortunate utterances. Under the crude phraseology of a "colored peril," for example, Spengler expresses something of the tragic cultural misunderstanding between Asia and the West—an incompatibility far transcending the clash of political institutions and economic interests. And beyond this inter-continental struggle, he sees the terrible outlines of a whole world delivered over to conquest and virtually perpetual war. He depicts the coming of an age of iron in which the traditional political issues, having lost any contemporary relevance, will have reduced themselves to a simple choice between technical expedients. He grasps the dilemma of creative endeavor in an era of mass culture—its fatal division between a merely repetitive popular art and the esoteric experiments of the "progressive" schools. And he understands the implications of mass culture itself. He sees what one of his German critics (using the American expression) calls the whole "phonyness" of contemporary life—the depressing uniformity of great city society and its deadening effect on democratic procedures. Finally, he comprehends the emptiness and despair that are leading so many of our contemporaries—the untutored and the highly sophisticated alike—to seek solace in a return to dogmatic religion.

Spengler's talent as an imaginative writer, however, and the accuracy of his major predictions do not exhaust, or even properly establish, his intellectual importance. It is somewhere between literature and prophecy that the *Decline* has made its most telling contribution. It is as symptom, as synthesis, as symbol of a whole age that Spengler's book remains one of the major works of our century. Indeed it has gained in stature as the passage of time has enabled us to place it in the context of the events of the past three decades and the further catastrophes that nearly all of us anticipate. For when everything else has been said, the *Decline* bulks largest as the massive concretization of a state of mind—the state of mind of an old society anticipating its end. And this—despite brief flurries of hope—has become the characteristic attitude of social observers and the general public alike, both in Europe and, more recently, in the United States. Hence, as imaginative literature, if not as history in the strict sense, *The Decline of the West* offers the nearest thing we have to a key to our times. It formulates more comprehensively than any other single book the modern *malaise* that so many feel and so few can express. It has become the classic summary of the now familiar pessimism of the twentieth-century West with regard to its own historical future.

Together Spengler's predictions, and the state of mind they express, set before us the emergence of a new barbarism. In them, we have learned to recognize our own era.

Suggestions for Further Reading

Western historical thought inherited four elements of friction: (1) A linear or (2) cyclical sense of motion, (3) cultural pessimism and/or primitivism, and (4) the idea of progress. Numbers one and two are mutually exclusive, but both may be combined with either three or four. Instead of playing a numbers game by pairing them off and picking sides, we ought to study their primary sources and face the ultimate issues.

The feeling of the shaky foundations, the futility of human existence, and the cultural pessimism which rocked the "cradle of Western civilization" may be recaptured by reading the creation and Gilgamesh epics, "I Will Praise the Lord of Wisdom" and "A Pessimistic Dialogue Between Master and Servant" in Isaac Mendelsohn, ed., *Religions of the Ancient Near East, Sumero-Akkadian Religious Texts and Ugaritic Epics* (Indianapolis, Ind., 1955).

Cultural and religious primitivism from the Cynics to Joachim of Floris can be pursued in A. O. Lovejoy, *et al., A Documentary History of Primitivism and Related Ideas in the Middle Ages* (Baltimore, 1935; reprinted, New York, 1965), and George Boas, *Essays on Primitivism and Related Ideas in the Middle Ages* (Baltimore, 1948; reprinted, New York, 1966). Johns Hopkins Press published a study by Lois Whitney, *Primitivism and the Idea of Progress in English Popular Literature of the Eighteenth Century* (Baltimore, 1934), which shows that the ideas of rise and fall are as interrelated as the two sides of a seesaw. Progressives and pessimists share the same sense of movement but differ on its upward or downward swing, both of which alternate in a cyclical view.

The books of Genesis, Amos, and Daniel in the Old Testament and the Revelation of St. John the Divine in the New Testament exhibit the Hebrew-Christian sense of history and mission. For the Hebrews, the form of history was genealogy *(toldoth);* its content, covenant *(b'rith).* History dealt with a chain of human beings—Adam, Noah, Abraham, Moses—who stood in a special relationship to the Holy One who had made man in his image and revealed himself by the way in which he preserved his people. There were no sacred animals as in Egypt nor holy planets as in Mesopotamia taking the place of the divine and distracting from human dignity. The proper story of mankind was man.

This anthropomorphism of the Western religious and historical heritage may explain the resistance to Spengler's morphology which implies a return to the sacred animals of Egypt and the holy planets of Mesopotamia. Although the Enlightenment submerged the Lord and his law into the "starry sky," and Darwinism made man part of the animal kingdom, traditional historians resent Spengler's analogies which parallel human destiny with the life of plants, as well as his occasional comparisons of the conduct of man with the behavior of beasts, but above all his historical cycles which reflect the paths of the planets and suggest that human destiny is predetermined like the course of the stars.

Was not the idea of progress by virtue of individual choice another mainstay of Hebrew history? Abraham left the star cult and nature worship of a city civilization in search of a personalized religion. Moses led his chosen people from an oppressive past toward a promising future. When they established another city civilization and fell prey to similar vices as the societies of Egypt and Mesopotamia, the prophet Amos tried to call them back to the desert. "If you do not obey the Law of the Lord, you will perish," insisted the prophets. Similar warnings did not only appear on the walls of Babylon but were echoed in more sophisticated terms by Schweitzer, Sorokin, or Toynbee.

When a faithful remnant reformed and its lot became worse, apocalyptic literature interpreted the rise and fall of civilizations as curtain raisers of the coming kingdom of God. This vision of eschatological progress pervades the book of Daniel and its Christian counterpart, the Revelation of St. John, as well as St. Augustine's *City of God* and the *History Against the Pagans* by Paulus Orosius. The Catholic University of America Press published new translations of the latter two books in 1962 and 1964 respectively. The last great advocate of this view was J. B. Bossuet, *Discours sur l'histoire universelle* (1681), which is contained in his *Oeuvres* (Paris, 1961).

If Orosius wrote his history against the pagans, Edward Gibbon aimed *The Decline and Fall of the Roman Empire* (best edition J. B. Bury, ed., London, 1896–1900 and 1909–1914) against the Christians.

In his "General Observations on the Fall of the Roman Empire in the West," Gibbon repeated the profession of faith which the pagan atheist Lucretius had made in *De rerum natura* (58 B.C.) shortly before Rome reached its peak, namely, that man would progress once he had banished religious barbarism, and reason enlightened his mind. Because this had been achieved once more by 1788, Gibbon believed a decline of the West would not happen again.

The related ideas of Voltaire and A. R. J. Turgot are summed up in de Condorcet's *Sketch for a Historical Picture of the Progress of the Human Mind* (London, 1955). An extension of de Condorcet, contemporaneous with Spengler, was *The Outline of History* (New York, 1921) by the English novelist Herbert George Wells, which was written with the advice of leading historians and went through many popular editions. Lovat

Dickson, *Friend of Man: The Turbulent Life and Times of H. G. Wells* (New York, 1969) reveals the passionate pessimism behind his disparate optimism and again recalls de Condorcet who produced his masterpiece in the shadow of death.

Among the ancients a cyclical pattern of history was implied by Herodotus, Plato, and Aristotle and espoused in the sixth book of *The Histories of Polybius* (Bloomington, 1962). *The Epitome of Roman History* by Lucius Annaeus Florus is published by the Loeb Classical Library (Cambridge, Mass., 1957) where Polybius can be found too. *The History of the Peloponnesian War* by Thucydides, edited by Sir Richard Livingstone (New York, 1960), should be also read in this context. In his editorial notes, Sir Richard considered the Peloponnesian War contemporaneous to World War II; Toynbee had felt it was much similar to World War I.

Apart from historical narratives, the cyclical view characteristically arose for the first time in a didactic poem on the "phainomena" of the stars and the sky. In a digression from his astronomy lessons Aratus of Soli (*c.* 275 B.C.) coupled the recurrence of Hesiod's four ages with the withdrawal and return of virtue symbolized by the constellation of the Virgin. *Phainomena* is published by the Loeb Classical Library (Cambridge, Mass.)

There is a new translation of *The New Science of Giambattista Vico* (Ithaca, 1948); an abridgment was published as an Anchor Book (New York, 1961). H. P. Adams, *The Life and Writings of Giambattista Vico* (London, 1935) may serve as Ariadne's thread through Vico's labyrinthine labors.

Straight as well as semicircular attempts at understanding civilizations include De Voltaire, *Philosophy of History* (New York, 1965) and his more serious and voluminous (2000 pages) *Essai sur les moeurs et l'ésprit de nations* (Paris, 1963). Easier to read and more rewarding are J. G. Herder, *Reflections on the Philosophy of the History of Mankind* (Chicago, 1968), G. W. Hegel, *Reason in History* (Indianapolis, Ind., 1953) or *Lectures on the Philosophy of History* (New York, 1956), A. Comte, *A General View of*

Positivism (Stanford, Calif., 1953), K. Marx, *The 18th Brumaire of Louis Bonaparte* (New York), according to which history repeats itself "the first time as tragedy, the second as farce," and F. S. C. Northrop, *The Meeting of East and West* (New York, 1946).

The first forerunner of Spengler, who tried to put this particular stream of historical consciousness into a system, was Carl Vollgraff, *Erster Versuch einer wissenschaftlichen Begründung sowohl der allgemeinen Ethnologie durch die Anthropologie wie auch der Staats- und Rechts-Philosophie durch die Ethnologie oder Nationalität der Völker* (Marburg, 1853–1855). Vollgraff explained how one should research and write such a comparative history of civilizations in *Wie muss man forschen und dann schreiben? nachgewiesen durch die Analyse des Werkes: Erster Versuch* and so on (Marburg, 1855). Because the *Erster Versuch* hardly sold any copies, the work was unsuccessfully reissued under the shorter title *Staats- und Rechtsphilosophie auf der Grundlage einer wissenschaftlichen Menschen- und Völkerkunde* (Frankfurt, 1864). On Vollgraff and his successor Lasaulx as well as Burckhardt, see Hans Joachim Schoeps, *Vorläufer Spenglers* (2d ed.; Leiden, 1955).·

Ernst von Lasaulx, *Neuer Versuch einer alten auf die Wahrheit der Tatsachen gegründeten Philosophie der Geschichte* (1856) has been re-edited by E. Thurnher (Munich, 1952). Another new edition of one of Lasaulx's works, *Der Untergang des Hellenismus* (Stuttgart, 1965), is a very readable and revealing illustration of his cyclical decline theory. Lasaulx's prophetic speeches can be found in his *Studien des classischen Althertums* (Regensburg, 1854), pp. 510–551.

The other Catholic conservative prophet, Donoso-Cortés, seems to be more honored in Germany than in his own country. There is a German edition of *Donoso-Cortés: Briefe, Reden und diplomatische Berichte* (Cologne, 1950) by A. Maier as well as a study by C. Schmitt, *Donoso-Cortés in gesamteuropäischer Interpretation* (Cologne, 1950), and a reprint of the translation of Donoso-Cortés, *Ensayo sobre el catolicismo, el liberalismo y el so-* *cialismo* entitled *Der Staat Gottes: Eine katholische Geschichtsphilosophie* (Darmstadt, 1966). The latest Spanish edition of his works was *Obras de Don Juan Donoso-Cortés* edited by J. Juretschke (Madrid, 1946).

Jakob Burckhardt's *Reflections on History* (London, 1943) were edited more completely as *Force and Freedom* (New York, 1943; Boston, 1964). Other lecture notes of his have been published with a laudatory introduction by H. R. Trevor-Roper under the title *On History and Historians* (New York, 1965).

The only access in a Western language to Danilevsky's book is the German translation *Russland und Europa* (Stuttgart and Berlin, 1920) which leaves out a few unimportant sections. On "The Question of Heinrich Rückert's Influence on Danilevskij," see the article by R. E. MacMaster in *The American Slavic and East European Review*, XIV (1955), 59–66. MacMaster also supplied an intellectual biography of *Danilevsky: A Russian Totalitarian Philosopher* (Boston, 1967).

Friedrich Nietzsche treated the tragic aspect of Greek culture in *The Birth of Tragedy out of the Spirit of Music*. The Modern Library edition (New York, 1927) of *The Philosophy of Nietzsche* offers under one cover *Thus Spake Zarathustra, Beyond Good and Evil, The Genealogy of Morals, Ecce Homo,* and *The Birth of Tragedy*. For flashes of insight into our time of troubles see *The Will to Power,* a new translation by Walter Kaufmann and R. J. Hollingdale (New York, 1968).

A work of fiction, which anticipated the totalitarianism of the twentieth century, was *The Devils* or *The Possessed Ones* by F. M. Dostoevski, on the market in various paperbacks. Georges Sorel, *Reflections on Violence* (New York, 1961) sounded also a "note from underground," although like Pareto in a lighter air.

The shortest and most readable introduction to Vilfredo Pareto's theory of "the circulation of elites" is *The Rise and Fall of the Elites* (Totowa, N.J., 1968), a translation of *Un applicazione di teorie sociologiche* (1901). Pareto's major work, *Treatise on General Sociology,* appeared as a reprint (New York, 1963).

From the books by Brooks Adams select *America's Economic Supremacy* (New York, 1900), republished with a new evaluation by M. W. Childs (London, 1947); *The New Empire* (New York, 1902); and, most important, *The Law of Civilization and Decay* (New York, 1896) which was reissued with an introduction by C. H. Beard (New York, 1951). *The Degradation of the Democratic Dogma* (New York, 1919; reprinted, 1949) and *The Education of Henry Adams* (New York, 1931) explain the latter's historical pessimism.

The writings of Oswald Spengler should be consulted in the revised edition of *Der Untergang des Abendlandes* (2 vols.; Munich, 1923–1924). An index to the first volume called *Namen- und Sachverzeichnis* appeared separately (Munich, 1923). *The Decline of the West* complete in one volume (New York, 1939) is an authorized translation by Charles Francis Atkinson. An English abridged edition prepared by Arthur Helps from the translation by C. H. Atkinson was published by The Modern Library (New York, 1965). There are two Gateway paperback editions of Spengler's *Aphorisms* and *Selected Essays* (Chicago, 1967).

A selective bibliography of works by and on Spengler can be found in H. Stuart Hughes, *Oswald Spengler* (2d rev. ed.; New York, 1962), pp. 169–171. Manfred Schröter, *Metaphysik des Unterganges* (Munich, 1949) contains the content of his earlier book, *Der Streit um Spengler* (Munich, 1922), in which he reviewed about four hundred of Spengler's critics. André Fauconnet, *Oswald Spengler* (Paris, 1925) is a patient explanation of the man and his work for those who read French. On Spengler and National Socialism, see H. S. Hughes, *Oswald Spengler* (New York, 1962), pp. 120–136 as well as H. J. Schoeps, *Vorläufer Spenglers*, pp. 96–97. Hans Frank, *Im Angesicht des Galgens* (Munich, 1953), p. 53, records that in 1924 Spengler described Hitler as the man who was "doing the business of Germany's enemies," and who would "destroy the *Reich*." Compare also pp. 31–33 and 255–258 of Frank's eye-witness account.

C. H. Meray published *Die Physiologie unserer Weltgeschichte und der kommende Tag* (Budapest, 1904), *Weltmutation* (Zurich, 1918), as well as a condensation of his doctrine, *Weltmutationstheorie* (Zurich, 1919).

Albert Schweitzer dealt with the "tragedy of the Western world" in his autobiography *Out of My Life and Thought* (New York, 1949), *The Philosophy of Civilization* (New York, 1949), and *Civilization and Ethics* (London, 1949).

If the twelve volumes of A. J. Toynbee, *A Study of History* (New York, 1934–1961) are too long, take the two-volume abridgment by D. C. Somervell (Oxford, 1947 and 1957), which is also out in paperback (New York, 1965). Of the original *Study*, read at least volume X, *The Inspirations of Historians*, and XII, *Reconsiderations*, in which Toynbee does himself what Schröter did for Spengler, that is, review the reviewers. *The Intent of Toynbee's History* (Chicago, 1961), edited by E. T. Gargan, is a worthwhile cooperative appraisal by ten specialists. Because Toynbee regarded "universal churches" as potential restorers of a divided world, *An Historian's Approach to Religion* (New York, 1956) and *Christianity among the Religions of the World* (New York, 1957) deserve special attention. *Civilization on Trial* (New York, 1948), *Acquaintances* (Oxford, 1967) and *Experiences* (Oxford, 1969) ought to round out the professional and personal picture of this popular historian.

Toynbee's most prominent and pronounced critics were Pieter Geyl and H. R. Trevor-Roper. Geyl's debate with Toynbee on the BBC in 1948, "Can We Know the Pattern of the Past?," appeared in *The Pattern of the Past* (Boston, 1949) under the names of the authors, together with two other evaluations, "Toynbee's System of Civilizations" by P. Geyl, and "Toynbee's Philosophy of History" by P. A. Sorokin. To appreciate Geyl's preoccupation with historiographical problems, which culminated in the critique of Spengler, Toynbee, and Sorokin, see *From Ranke to Toynbee* (vol. XXXIV; Northampton, Mass., 1952), *Use and Abuse of History* (New Haven, Conn., 1955), *Debates with Historians* (Cleveland, 1958), and *Encounters in History* (Cleveland, 1961). H. R. Trevor-

Roper, "Arnold Toynbee's Millennium," *Encounter* (June 1957), reprinted in *Encounters* selected by M. J. Lasky (New York, 1963), pp. 131–151, is an amusing mixture of vituperation and ridicule.

Two pertinent translations from N. Berdyaev's inexhaustible work are *The Meaning of History* (Cleveland, 1962) and *Towards a New Epoch* (London, 1949). Among W. Schubart's books, *Europa und die Seele des Ostens* (Lucerne, 1938), English title, *Russia and Western Man* (New York, 1950), *Dostojewski und Nietzsche* (Lucerne, 1939), and *Geistige Wandlung* (Lucerne, 1940) have a profound bearing on the decline of the West.

A survey of P. A. Sorokin should begin with his *Social Philosophies of an Age of Crisis* (Boston, 1950) which analyzes the works of Danilevsky, Spengler, Toynbee, Schubart, Berdyaev, F. S. C. Northrop, Kroeber, and Schweitzer and then measures them by Sorokin's standards underlining their areas of agreement as well as the importance of having a social philosophy in an age of crisis. To see whether Sorokin had his hand on the pulse of his time, read *The Crisis of Our Age* (New York, 1941), *The American Sex Revolution* (Boston, 1957), and *The Basic Trends of Our Times* (New Haven, Conn., 1964). Sorokin's experiences and acquaintances are reflected in *A Long Journey* (New Haven, Conn., 1963) which also includes "leaves from a Russian diary." F. R. Cowell, *History, Civilization and Culture* (London, 1952) is a good introduction to the historical and social philosophy of Sorokin. *Pitirim A. Sorokin in Review*, edited by J. P. Allen (Durham, N.C., 1963), contains "Sociology of My Mental Life" and "Reply to My Critics" by Sorokin as well as assessments of his insights and influences by sixteen international authorities.

A. L. Kroeber contributed to the organic philosophy of history with *Configurations of Culture Growth* (University of California Press, 1944), *Style and Civilizations* (Ithaca, N.Y., 1957) and *An Anthropologist Looks At History* (University of California Press, 1963) which epitomizes his viewpoints.

One measure of an intellectual movement's success is the number of those who follow in its footsteps. In 1926 Egon Friedell acknowledged a major debt to the model of Spengler in writing his *Cultural History of the Modern Age*. In the United States the three-volume work was translated by Spengler's translator, C. H. Atkinson, and published by his publisher, Alfred A. Knopf (New York, 1930–1932; reprinted 1933 and 1953–1954). In Germany Friedell is still a favorite of undergraduates.

In 1935 the founding of a scholarly journal, *Die Welt als Geschichte*, was inspired by Spengler's understanding of universal history. Today, it is edited by H. E. Stier and F. Ernst and is published in Stuttgart.

In 1954 Luis Diez del Corral, a countryman of Donoso-Cortés and Ortega y Gasset, paid tribute to pluralistic historiography, the cyclical concept of history, nineteenth-century pessimism, and the idea of decadence as correct expositions of the present situation. His *Rape of Europe* (New York, 1959) should be read side by side with Schubart, *Russia and Western Man*. One sees Europe from her Western frontier, the other from her Eastern frontier. But when it comes to Spain, their views are strikingly similar. Compare also Alfred Weber, *Farewell to European History* (London, 1947).

The Modern Approach to History (Jullundur, 1963) by the "Indian Toynbee" Buddha Prakash promoted the theories of historical change by Danilevsky, Spengler, Toynbee, Sorokin, Schubart, Berdyaev, Kroeber, Schweitzer, and Bagby (to be mentioned shortly). Prakash added his own "rhythm of activity-sleep-awakening" to them and discussed also the consciousness of decline in the ancient world, Moslem countries, India, China, and Japan.

On the American scene Eric Voegelin, professor of political science in Munich, Germany, has published four of six projected volumes entitled *Order and History* (Baton Rouge, La., 1956–1957). The late Crane Brinton hailed Voegelin as equal to Toynbee and Spengler. Philip Bagby, a student of Kroeber, contributed *Culture and History: Prolegomena to the Comparative Study of Civilizations* (London, 1958). Amaury Riencourt caused some controversy with *The Coming Caesars*

(New York, 1957). He correlated Europe with ancient Greece, and America with ancient Rome. He juxtaposed the decline of Europe with the rise of America. The West had spent its springtime of cultural growth in Europe and would reap its civilizational harvest in America. The Caesars with "armies of millions of men, the most powerful fleets in the world, commitments all over the globe, and vast nuclear power" could only come from a society where all were born equal and needed the projection of a mighty superego to identify themselves.

Herbert J. Muller, *The Uses of the Past* (New York, 1952) converted the cultural units of Spengler and Toynbee into "profiles of former societies," turned their periods of rise and fall into tables of virtues and vices, and lengthened the circular shadows of the past into an undulating line of progress leaving a sense of the irony and tragedy of history. If, in the context of our school, "Toynbee has been likened to St. Augustine, Muller may be compared to Gibbon," concluded H. S. Hughes.

William H. McNeill, *The Rise of the West* (Chicago, 1963), heartily endorsed by both Toynbee and Trevor-Roper, comes around full circle and reverses the decline theory. Western civilization returns to the center of the stage and other cultures offer challenging side shows to which the West responds by providing universal progress. The place of Western civilization within the curriculum of the American university will certainly be challenged by upcoming African, Asian, and American-Indian studies, a contest destined to enrich our concepts of culture and world history.

Theodore H. Von Laue, *The Global City: Freedom, Power, and Necessity in the Age of World Revolutions* (Philadelphia, 1969), as well as the "final report of the national commission on the causes and prevention of violence" entitled *To Establish Justice, To Insure Domestic Tranquility* (U.S. Government Printing Office, December 1969) bring the dilemmas and dimensions of our universal urban crisis up to date and place them in front of your doorsteps.